Transatlantic Lives

Rev. James McGregor's headstone, Forest Hill Cemetery, East Derry, NH

Transatlantic Lives
The Irish Experience in Colonial America

Edited by

Linde Lunney

James Quinn

William Roulston

ULSTER HISTORICAL FOUNDATION

COVER IMAGE

An accurate map of the British Empire in Nth. America as settled by the preliminaries in 1762 (Lionel Pincus and Princess Firyal Map Division, The New York Public Library).

Published 2019, reprinted 2022
by Ulster Historical Foundation
www.ancestryireland.com
www.booksireland.org.uk

ISBN: 978-1-909556-64-5

DESIGN AND FORMATTING
FPM Publishing

COVER DESIGN
J.P. Morrison

PRINTED BY
Lightning Source

Contents

Preface and acknowledgements

The idea for this book came from Dr Linde Lunney of the Dictionary of Irish Biography, Royal Irish Academy, who suggested that the publication of a volume of biographies selected from the Dictionary of Irish Biography would highlight the importance of the first great surge of emigration from Ireland to North America, which started with the migration of families from the Bann and Foyle valleys in the north of the island to New England in 1718. The project was supported by colleagues in the Dictionary and by the Board of the Dictionary of Irish Biography. The Ulster Historical Foundation was very happy to take on the role of publisher of the proposed volume. Cambridge University Press, the publisher of the *Dictionary of Irish Biography* (9 volumes, 2009), kindly gave permission for the selected biographies to be reproduced. The present book is the work of many hands; the authors of individual biographies are named at the end of each entry. To them and to everyone else involved in this enterprise we express our sincere thanks. A special acknowledgment is due to Dr Patrick Griffin, Madden-Hennebry Professor of History in the University of Notre Dame, and Director, Keough-Naughton Institute for Irish Studies, who supplied the introductory essay.

DR LINDE LUNNEY, formerly Royal Irish Academy

DR JAMES QUINN, Royal Irish Academy

DR WILLIAM ROULSTON, Ulster Historical Foundation

Editors' note
on the selection of biographies

This volume features fifty-nine biographical essays from the Royal Irish Academy's Dictionary of Irish Biography (DIB), published online and in nine hard-copy volumes by Cambridge University Press in 2009, detailing the careers of a selection of Irish emigrants to North America in the colonial period (including the British territories that would later become Canada). Those chosen are a representative sample of some of the more notable figures among these emigrants. Colonial administrators, soldiers and clergymen predominate. Among clergymen, Presbyterians (of various hues) are the most numerous, but space has also been found for Methodists, Anglicans and Catholics, all of whom made their contribution to shaping the religious culture of the colonies.

The selection, however, also includes educators, doctors, writers, artists, printers, merchants and even a (female) pirate to give some sense of the diversity of such emigrants, and their varying contributions to the economic and cultural development of the colonies. Most of these stayed in the colonies, but a sufficient number returned to Ireland, providing some evidence for the contention that emigration to the colonies was not always an irrevocable decision.

The volume focuses primarily on those who emigrated during the eighteenth century, several of whom played notable parts in the events leading up to the American War of Independence (1775–83) and the subsequent founding of the United States of America. The selection here reminds us, however, that not all the Irish who went to the colonies were emigrants; some were sent by the British government as administrators or career soldiers. And not all Irish emigrants supported American independence; a number of those featured in this volume were Loyalists.

Where place of birth can be determined, Ulster is well represented, as might be expected, especially counties Antrim, Londonderry and Donegal, although the provinces of Leinster and Munster also feature strongly, indicating that eighteenth-century emigration to America was clearly not just an Ulster phenomenon. Emigration has continued ever since, and the lives of Irish men and women have had an immense and lasting impact on the development of North America.

Monument to Major-General Robert Ross, Rostrevor, Co. Down

Abbreviations

Allibone	S. A. Allibone, *Critical dictionary of English literature and British and American authors living and deceased* (3+2 vols, Philadelphia and London, 1859)
ANB	*American National Biography*, ed. J. A. Garraty and M. C. Carnes (New York and Oxford, 1999)
Appletons	*Appletons' cyclopedia of American biography*, ed. James Grant Wilson and John Fiske (6 vols, New York, 1887–9); *The cyclopedia of American biography, supplementary edition* (5 vols, New York 1924–8)
BBA	*British Biographical Archive*
DAB	*Dictionary of American Biography*, ed. Allen Johnson and Dumas Malone (22 vols [to 31 Dec. 1940], New York and London, 1928–58; reissued in 11 vols, New York, 1955–64; supplementary vols for 1941 and after)
DCB	*Dictionary of Canadian Biography* (Toronto and London, 1966–)
DNB	*The Dictionary of National Biography*, ed. Sir Leslie Stephen and Sir Sidney Lee (66 vols, London, 1885–1901)
McConnell, *Fasti*	James McConnell, *Fasti of the Irish Presbyterian Church, 1613–1840*, revised by Samuel G. McConnell (12 fascs, Belfast, 1951)
ODNB	*Oxford Dictionary of National Biography*, ed. H. C. G. Matthew and Brian Harrison (60 vols, Oxford, 2004)
Webb	Alfred Webb, *A compendium of Irish biography* (Dublin, 1878)

List of biographies

Place of birth in Ireland
(where known)

Places in USA and Canada
associated with individuals

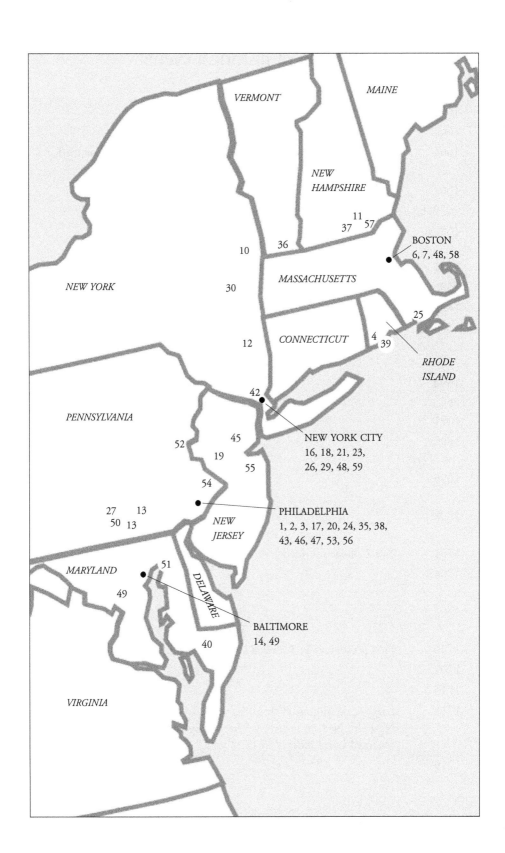

VERMONT

MAINE

NEW
HAMPSHIRE

11
37   57

10   36

BOSTON
6, 7, 48, 58

NEW YORK

30

MASSACHUSETTS

25

12

CONNECTICUT

4
39

RHODE
ISLAND

42

PENNSYLVANIA

45

52

19

55

54

27   13
50   13

NEW
JERSEY

NEW YORK CITY
16, 18, 21, 23,
26, 29, 48, 59

PHILADELPHIA
1, 2, 3, 17, 20, 24, 35, 38,
43, 46, 47, 53, 56

MARYLAND

51

DELAWARE

49

40

BALTIMORE
14, 49

VIRGINIA

Timeline of historical events

Date	North America
1660	
1663	Charter issued creating colony of Carolina
1664	New Netherland annexed by British; New Amsterdam renamed New York
1667	
1679–80	New Hampshire separated from Massachusetts
1680s	
1681	Pennsylvania granted to William Penn by Charles II
1686	Charter for New York City granted
1688	
1689	
1690	
1691	
1690s	
1695	
1698	
1701	Yale College founded
1704	
1705	
1706	First presbytery in America convened in Philadelphia
1707	
1715	
1718	Large-scale migration from the north of Ireland to New England; Nutfield, NH, founded by Ulster-Scots in 1719; renamed Londonderry in 1722
1719	

Ireland and Great Britain	Biography
Restoration of monarchy	
Ban on cattle exports from Ireland to England	
The 'Killing Time' in Scotland: Covenanters persecuted by government	
	Penn
	Dongan
The 'Glorious Revolution' sees James II deposed	
William of Orange declared king	
Siege of Derry (Apr.–July)	Clerk
	McGregor
Battle of the Boyne (1 July)	
Formation of the Presbyterian general synod of Ulster	
Treaty of Limerick ends Williamite War in Ireland (Oct.)	
Severe famine conditions in Scotland; many families move to Ulster	
The first of the penal laws restricting Catholic rights passed by the Irish parliament	
The first Scottish colonists arrive at the Isthmus of Panama as part of the ill-fated Darien scheme	
Sacramental test extended to Ireland: civil and military office restricted to Anglicans	
English parliament allowed Irish linen to be exported direct to colonies	
	Makemie
Act of Union between England and Scotland	
Unsuccessful Jacobite rising in Scotland	
	Boyd
	Clerk
	McGregor
The Toleration Act gives some recognition to Ireland's Dissenters	

Date	North America
1720	
1725–6	
1728	
1729	North and South Carolina officially become Crown colonies
1732	Charter of Georgia Colony
1733	
1730s/40s	Religious revival known as the 'Great Awakening'
1740–41	
1741	First expedition to find a north-west passage; second expedition in 1746–7; both failures
1743	Renewal of Solemn League and Covenant at Octorara, PA
1745–6	
1746	College of New Jersey (later Princeton University) founded
1747	
1755	Academy of Philadelphia becomes the College of Philadelphia (University in 1779)
1756–63	Seven Years' War between Britain and France (known as the French and Indian War in America)
1758	Reunification of the two Presbyterian synods
1759	France cedes Canada to Britain
1760	
1761	First attempt to establish an Ulster colony in Nova Scotia
1762	First St Patrick's Day parade in New York City (17 Mar.)
1763	
1765	Stamp Act (22 Mar.) fuelled considerable discontent among colonists
1771	Society of Friendly Sons of St Patrick founded in Philadelphia

Ireland and Great Britain	Biography
The 'South Sea Bubble' bursts, resulting in financial catastrophe	
Subscription controversy within Irish Presbyterianism reaches a climax with the formation of the Presbytery of Antrim	Clerk
Catholics in Ireland denied the vote	
Several Irish Presbyterian ministers petition the king about the departure for America of so many of their co-religionists	Craghead
The Corboy exodus of families from Co. Longford and adjoining districts; the emigrants settle in Ulster County, NY, in 1731	Dobbs Clinton
Associate Presbytery (Seceders) formed in Scotland; first Seceder minister ordained in Ireland in 1746	Clark
	Craghead
Severe famine in Ireland	Tennent (all)
	Dobbs
	Craghead
Unsuccessful Jacobite rising in Scotland	
	Tennent (Gilbert) Finley
John Wesley made the first of many visits to Ireland	Embury Heck Alison
	Carleton Caldwell Clinton Dobbs Johnson (Wm) Montgomery Alison Tennent (Gilbert) Caldwell
Carrickfergus captured by French force led by Francois Thurot	Jackson
First Reformed Presbytery established in Ireland	Martin Alison
	Fitzsimons

Date	North America
1772	
1773	Boston Tea Party (16 Dec.)
1774	Catholics in Canada granted civil and religious rights
	Meeting of First Continental Congress (5 Sep.)
1775	Beginning of War of Independence (Apr.)
	Battle of Quebec (Dec.)
1776	Declaration of Independence (4 July)
1778	
1780	
1781	Surrender of Cornwallis at Yorktown (19 Oct.)
1782	
1783	Treaty of Paris signed by British (3 Sep.)
1784	US Congress approves the Treaty of Paris (14 Jan.)
1785	Dollar adopted as the US currency
1787	US Constitution prepared (Sep.); ratified 1788
1789	House of Representatives meets for the first time (1 Apr.)
1790	Washington approved for the new capital
1791	Canada Act passed in London (10 June)
	US Bill of Rights (15 Dec.)

Ireland and Great Britain	Biography
Large exodus of families from Co. Antrim to South Carolina	Martin
Act allows Irish Catholics to pledge allegiance to Crown	Carleton
	Thomson
	Barry
	Caldwell
	Carleton
	Fitzsimons
	Gaine
	Inglis
	Jackson
	Johnson (Guy)
	McHenry
	Montgomery
	Moylan
	Pollock
	Dunlap
	Taylor
	Thomson
	Thornton
Rise of the Volunteer movement in Ireland	
US ship *Ranger* defeats HMS *Drake* in the mouth of Belfast Lough (Apr.)	
First Catholic relief act in Ireland (Aug.)	
Sacramental test repealed in Ireland	
Legislative independence conceded to Irish parliament	
Further Catholic relief act in Ireland (May)	
Irish Presbyterian marriages recognised as valid	
	Pollock
	Dunlap
	McHenry
	Paterson
Society of United Irishmen founded in Belfast (14 Oct.)	Burk
	Caldwell
	O'Donel

Introduction

Putting eighteenth-century Irish migration to America in context

Patrick Griffin

The Irish migrants of the seventeenth and eighteenth centuries were both products and producers of an early modern globalizing process, one that remade the Ireland they left and the America to which they ventured. In playing these roles, they stood at the centre of some of the most momentous dynamics and events in world history. They helped turn the Atlantic from a watery space or barrier between Old and New Worlds into an integrated system, both by moving across it and by producing and consuming the goods that knit it together. Through peopling the Continent, Irish migrants participated in the expulsion of native Americans to pave the way for what people in the eighteenth century hailed as the 'improvement' of surplus land for production. Some were complicit in enslaving Africans as a labour force. The Irish in America provided many of the thinkers who worked to make sense of these seismic changes. Finally, they fought in the global wars for dominance of that system, as well, even more critically, in the revolutions to which these wars contributed.[1]

Fairly heady stuff for a people often deemed faceless and perhaps even nameless.[2] Truth be told, though, they did not prove exceptional, as some ethnic hagiographers would have us believe. In fact, they typified a century that witnessed the transformation of both Europe and America through growing entanglements. If they played outsized roles in this process, they did so because of sheer numbers. The selections in this volume point to the people we remember. They are the notables. But they represent only a sliver of all those who travelled to America in the 'long eighteenth century'. Most remained anonymous. Most farmed. Some traded. Most lived upstanding lives, working to keep body and soul together and striving to raise families. Many proved mobile, some moving a number of times. All lived during a tumultuous and exhilarating period, roughly straddling the Glorious Revolution, when Ireland was bound more closely to Britain, and the period of the Early Republic in the United States, when all Atlantic peoples were struggling with an age of revolution. The men and women we remember, however, those in the volume, offer glimpses of the changing world all the migrants from Ireland to America had to negotiate.

Let us start with what we know and do not know. To begin with, numbers are not easy to come by. From 1717, when large-scale movement began, until the War of Independence, anywhere between 50,000 and 250,000 men and women set sail from Irish ports for British North America. Most likely, somewhere around 150,000 left before the Revolution.[3] Migration to the new republic began soon after the period of revolution in America, and numbers picked up until the Napoleonic Wars. We figure 60,000 left between 1783 and 1799.[4] The numbers for this later period appear reliable.

Where they left and where they went are easier to pin down. Simply put, most departed where ships were sailing from, and went to the ports they were sailing to. Migration, then, was tied to systemic imperatives. Let us start with exceptions. Some of the earliest Presbyterian migrants ventured to New England, where they expected a decent welcome from fellow Calvinists. Now the rule: in most cases throughout the century, most ventured, first, to the Middle Colonies, including New York, or the upper Chesapeake colony of Maryland. Later, a significant movement would take place to South Carolina. Throughout these years, Pennsylvania, serviced by Philadelphia and New Castle in Delaware, stood as the place of choice for most migrants. Many stayed where they landed, and large communities of men and women from Ireland settled in the city of Philadelphia; a larger number continued to move. The patterns for those landing in the Delaware River ports and, after the Seven Years' War in Baltimore, are unmistakable. Once again, they sailed where ships were destined.

Most went in search of land they could work, purchase, or settle on with an eye toward improving and acquiring, in a sequence of regions as the century progressed. Settlement reflected these imperatives. Earliest migrants headed to southeast Pennsylvania to what would be Lancaster County. Later arrivals leapfrogged these to establish themselves over the Susquehanna River, beginning in the late 1730s. The next wave landed in the same ports but headed further south on what was quickly becoming a 'great wagon road' in the Shenandoah Valley of Virginia. Others entered southern ports and travelled still further south along the edge of Appalachians to the backcountry of North and South Carolina.[5]

This simple survey of movement barely captures what was happening to the Atlantic in these years and how the Irish brought it into being. Migrants came from all over Ireland because of how the kingdom was enmeshed in a broader process of British state formation, beginning with the Glorious Revolution, and how all of the kingdom was tied imaginatively and materially into a dynamic trading system. Ireland's immersion was mediated by the imperatives of commercial expansion and British imperial reach. To be sure, Catholics, churchmen, Quakers, and later Methodists all sailed. Just take a look, for instance, at James Logan. Logan was one of a large number of Friends who left the British Isles to sustain the network of trade that would build Philadelphia into a centre of Atlantic commerce. He also played an important role in recruiting settlers from Ireland to settle on the frontier as 'a hedge' against native Americans, and so pushing the bounds of the colony further west. William Johnson also ended up moving to the frontiers, and this man who had been born a Catholic in Meath would become the most important British official on the American frontier and would be adopted by the Mohawk as one of their own. Johnson would have a hand in the expansion of British imperial power to the very edges of the frontier. Philip Embury led a group of Methodists involved in the linen trade in Limerick to settle in New York. Here they facilitated the further integration of Ireland and the American colonies, both in terms of commerce and religion. In his group travelled Barbara Heck, the so-called 'Mother of Methodism'.

Nonetheless, Presbyterians from Ulster outnumbered all others, but not because these people were somehow providentially suited for journeying to the frontier and serving at the vanguard of American settlement. Far from it. These people predominated because of how deeply enmeshed they were into the changing Atlantic system. These people moved from regions dynamically changing in Ireland in the wake of the Glorious Revolution to some of the most dynamic places in America. Ulster, through the production of linen, was tied more securely than any other Irish province into the Atlantic economy. It also explains why Presbyterians outnumbered those of other faiths. Their ancestors had settled that region of Ireland as a part of a process of British state formation within the archipelago. The multi-generational story of these people is fascinating, demonstrating how the complex links between Ireland, Scotland, and then America were forged by British state power and Atlantic commercial dynamism. Later, all of Ireland, including the west, would be drawn into the British-mediated Atlantic system, especially when it reached an industrial scale, but in the eighteenth century, Ulster was tied more perfectly into it. In this volume, many of the notables descended from those who had left Scotland in the seventeenth century as part of settlement schemes in Ulster or because of famine and political instability. Many of these were really part of a marchland movement between the British Isles and from these places to America. They were 'a people with no name,' but they had a great deal in common with Scots, another marchland people affected by the extension of the British state to the margins and who would leave directly for America after 1750. Indeed, perhaps a better way of conceiving movement between the British Isles and the American colonies in the eighteenth century would be to consider it a 'Scots/Irish' pattern.[6]

The Atlantic narrative also explains specifically where people settled. Philadelphia had become America's most significant Atlantic hub for the mid-eighteenth century. Understandably, the numbers streaming to New England remained low after the initial burst of movement there, as Boston languished throughout much of the eighteenth century. Not so three other cities that would, with Philadelphia, come of age through Atlantic integration. New York would become a centre after the Seven Years' War, as would Baltimore. Charleston also attracted some, once it was transformed into an Atlantic entrepôt because of its dominance of a very different trade: the slave trade. Many stayed in these places. But many did not. From these ports, thousands then moved to backcountry regions. The frontier regions of Pennsylvania, then the Shenandoah Valley of Virginia, and afterward the backcountry of the Carolinas were places that were increasingly bound to a broader world of migration and of trade. Far from marginal, as they would later become, these places tied the productive capacity of the North American interior into the Atlantic economy.

Where the Irish went, a land-rich New World met a land-poor Old World, and a labour-hungry America was bound to a labour-saturated Ireland. Their bodies bound this world together. With each farm set up, with each foray by a trader further and further west, the Atlantic was further shaped into a system with integrity. The ships that migrants sailed, and that transported linen from Ireland and crops from America, formed a complex network of comings and goings that transformed the space and presented all with new challenges and opportunities. Through their work, their movement, what they grew and made, and what they consumed, the Atlantic Irish served as midwives to a transition from an Atlantic that functioned as a salt-water barrier to one that worked as a highway.[7]

Notables and faceless alike animated the Atlantic. Some did so by exploiting the interstices between imperial realms in a deeply entangled Atlantic system. The pirate Anne Bonney was one. She was hardly alone, of course, as the Irish had their fair share of those who tried to take advantage of what the system had to offer. Many did so by looking for connections within this world. Clergymen offer a prime example, as Ireland and much of America were bound together in the same religious and intellectual world. Francis Makemie, the so-called father of American Presbyterianism, comes to mind. So, too, the earliest adventurers to New England, like James McGregor, Matthew Clerk, and William Boyd. But many others did as well. The Irish sent traders and merchants, soldiers and speculators. If the eighteenth-century Atlantic was brought into being by the mobility of people, goods, and ideas, the Irish had a hand in all three. Arthur Dobbs, to name just the most famous, would serve as a facilitator of the system, establishing settlements and recruiting the Irish to North Carolina.

The Irish also sent those who tried to make sense of the new possibilities of the Atlantic by what they wrote. Atlantic integration confronted all with intellectual challenges and possibilities, forcing all to creatively reimagine older ways. These challenges ranged from new wealth to understanding the status of exploited groups. How should the ideals of the individual be weighed against the demands of the whole? How could the mastery of some over others be justified? A group of scholars who had cut their teeth on Irish questions in Ireland before going to America engaged in these timely debates in the New World. These included world-famous luminaries such as George Berkeley. Francis Alison discussed these tensions in religious terms, but he was essentially involved in a series of debates about the rights of the individual versus the rights of community in determining orthodoxy. A man of the enlightenment, he also held to more formal understandings of theology. He had a hand in creating an institution where such debates could take place, what would become the University of Pennsylvania. A more radical proponent of enlightenment ideals was Samuel Hemphill. Hemphill, whom Benjamin Franklin regarded as a model man of God, preached a new form of religious experience, one that was tied into the enlightened currents of the day and posited that reason could provide a path of salvation. His was a faith ideally suited to a changing world.

He was arrayed against those who supported the 'new light' vision of piety. The story of the Great Awakening does not need recounting here, but some of the leaders of the new light movement, many in fact, came from Ireland. The most famous were Gilbert Tennent and Samuel Finley. In American textbooks, they emerge as two of the most prominent purveyors of a new vital piety also well suited to a new age. But rather than see these in narrow religious terms, we would be wise to see the Awakening as a distinctive Irish-inflected American response to many changes gripping the colonies in the wake of Atlantic consolidation. What was a community in a world defined by mobility? Should an individual determine his or her own religiosity? And what was the relationship between material things – the goods that came in ships – and relationship to God? In many ways, this path to God, based on individual experience but pushing back against the excesses of the age, was tailor-made for the changing world as well. The Irish, who made the world they needed to navigate, stood at the heart of such debates.

They also played critical roles in raising the imperial stakes in this integrated space. Between 1754 and 1763, Britain and France went to war for dominance of the system, and the Irish were involved. About one-third of British troops who fought in the Seven Years' War were Irish.[8] Many of them went on to serve in America and some of them re-established their lives there thereafter. Richard Montgomery was one. So, too, was Henry Caldwell. Guy Carleton would lead troops in America, then would become one of Britain's most important officials in America. Men like these made up a small part of a much broader dynamic determined by Atlantic integration. All powers had to try to manage or profit from the Atlantic if they were to compete successfully. The Seven Years' War was touched off as more and more men and women, many of them Irish, began streaming into the colonies and began pushing west looking for land and opportunity. The British state tried to harness and control this movement, channelling it to places like the Ohio River Valley, where hostilities first broke out. And officials also placed such people in harm's way because the French claimed such regions as well. Some Irish were able to take advantage of the state of affairs, and used the ensuing war as an opportunity for advancement. Think here of characters featured in this volume, such as William Johnson. A jack of many trades, he exploited native Americans, even as he lived as one of them. He worked as a frontier trader, tying hinterlands to the Atlantic. He owned slaves. He became Britain's first hero in the Seven Years' War.

The Irish, unsurprisingly, would play outsized roles in the Atlantic-wide crisis that followed the war. The broad drama is well known. European states now sought to implement sweeping reforms in the wake of the war, all to tie centres and peripheries more closely together and to ease the debt the war brought on. The British did so more thoroughly than others. And the familiar litany of events – from Stamp Act, to Townshend Duties crisis, to Boston Massacre, to Tea Party, and Intolerable or Coercive Acts – formed the very stuff of British attempts to create a transatlantic system to rationalize integration. Provincials, of course, pushed back to maintain as much autonomy as they could. The Irish in America tended to support the patriots in resisting what parliament was doing. They did so not only because an 'Irish rebellion' against British authority was taking place in America.[9] They sided with American creoles against established authority for many reasons. They did so because, as a people who shaped the Atlantic economy, they now wanted to profit by their efforts. Sometimes it had to do with local contexts, and regions where the Irish settled tended to be pro-patriot, unlike, say, where Scots tended to live. Sometimes it had to do with money. At other times, ideological patterns mattered. No ideas championed by patriots – think of 'no taxation without representation' – could have surprised the Irish who had long tussled with such tensions. But if we step back and look at the big picture, resistance, for the Irish, made sense. After all, they tended to be about the most dynamic, forward-looking people in the Atlantic society. They had to be, coming as they were from a marginalized kingdom in the archipelago. And what American patriots were calling for, ideals premised on the enjoyment of rights to life, liberty, and the pursuit of happiness, mimicked the very Atlantic lives so many of them led.

Unsurprisingly, a number of Irish would sign the document that would announce these words to the world. The Irishmen James Smith and George Taylor put their names on the Declaration of Independence. And, of course, John Dunlap printed the document. Their stories are all here in the volume. Just as impressive are those who fought for the American side in the war. Indeed, the Irish, like Charles Clinton who had been a vocal supporter of the British Crown during the Seven Years' War, would become some of the most visible fighters for the patriot cause shortly thereafter. And some played prominent roles. John Barry, Richard Montgomery, William Irvine, and Stephen Moylan, just to name a very few, are remembered to this day as leading patriots. Montgomery was hailed, in fact, as the first patriot martyr of the cause after leading the failed invasion of Canada. Barry is considered 'the father of the American navy.' Irvine would serve as a prominent commander of patriot forces in the West. Moylan, whose brother was a bishop in Cork, came from a prominent trading family in Ireland and would become one of Washington's most trusted aides. These sorts outnumbered Loyalists, such as perhaps the most famous American opponent to the patriot cause, the Irishman Charles Inglis, by a substantial margin. But it was again those, whose individual stories have been forgotten, who really mattered. The Pennsylvania Line during the revolutionary war was so heavily Irish in composition that it was rightly called 'the Line of Ireland'.[10]

The Irish would unsurprisingly continue to feature after the war. Ireland and America were still imaginatively bound to one another. In some cases, as revolution spread far and wide to many places, including Ireland, these ties would be amplified. And so, one of the most significant movements after the Revolution witnessed many United Irish émigrés heading to places like New York and Philadelphia. These Atlantic refugees wanted to keep the promise of the age alive. If Ireland could not be a republic, perhaps the United States could be a more just one. Many of their names are well known, but for a good example refer to the biography here of John Daly Burk. Others, such as Matthew Lyon, who were inspired by transatlantic radicalism also played outsized roles in American political culture after the Revolution. Once again, these men are representative of broader Irish participation in American political life during the early republic. Jefferson's Democratic Republicans, after all, had a heavily Irish-inflected composition.[11]

After the Revolution, Irish migration to America would pick up again. But once again it was the many faceless men and women, not only the radical émigrés, that sailed. They would follow an old pattern, as most would depart the most dynamically changing places of Ireland for those regions in America entangled with the Atlantic system. In this case, many would leave south Ulster and north Leinster, those areas quickly being transformed by immersion in a broader market economy, for the most dynamic places in the United States. Many of them were heading to growing cities, those places binding American hinterlands into the Atlantic economy. The unskilled also sought to work on sites that tied the North American Continent to the Atlantic. The Irish were the ones, after all, who built the canals and the bridges that served as the very embodiments and linchpins of early industrial Atlantic development.

The Irish story of the eighteenth century, therefore, makes no sense if it is untethered from the Atlantic. It just so happens that a people ideally suited to adaptation set sail at a moment in which a whole global system was changing, a transformation this same people had a hand in. It is not a coincidence that they would, then, find themselves in a crisis brought about by that systemic change, one that created world war and then revolutions that remade the political and social configurations of both the Old and New World. The outcomes of this seismic crisis would, if anything deepen the connections between Ireland and America, even if these places that had been politically conjoined through a British empire were now politically separated.

The nineteenth century would have a similar appearance, even if we have difficulty recognizing it as such. Ireland and America remained parts of the same intensely networked world. The nature of these networks, one seamlessly tying the demand of North America for labour to the surplus of peoples of the Old World, would make for the next great sets of connections and movements between Ireland and America. Famine, alas, would be cause of, symptom of, and accelerant to this process. Ironically, it would be the migration of millions of Catholic tenant farmers and labourers from places like the west of Ireland to American cities that would make the descendants of those earlier migrants forget or sanitise the distinctive ways that Ireland and America had been connected to each other from the period before the American Revolution.

Notes

1 For a look at this broader narrative, see Nicholas Canny and Philip Morgan's 'Introduction' to the *Oxford handbook of Atlantic history, 1450–1850* (New York, 2011). Bernard Bailyn calls the migration aspect one of the most significant developments in world history in *The peopling of British North America: an introduction* (New York, 1988).

2 Patrick Griffin, *The people with no name: Ireland's Ulster Scots, America's Scots Irish, and the creation of a British Atlantic world* (Princeton, 2001).

3 R. J. Dickson, *Ulster emigration to colonial America* (London, 1966); see also
   Graeme Kirkham's comments in his 'New Introduction' to the 1988 edition of
   Dickson's book (Belfast) as well as in his essay 'Ulster emigration to North
   America, 1680–1720,' in H. T. Blethen and C. W. Wood (ed.), *Ulster and
   North America: transatlantic perspectives on the Scotch-Irish* (Tuscaloosa, AL,
   1997), pp 76–117.

4 M. J. Bric, *Ireland, Philadelphia and the re-invention of America, 1760–1800*
   (Dublin, 2008); and the introduction (by Miller) in Kerby A. Miller, Arnold
   Schrier, Bruce D. Boling, David N. Doyle (ed.), *Irish immigrants in the land
   of Canaan: letters and memoirs from colonial and revolutionary America,
   1675–1815* (New York, 2003).

5 The latest work to explore this movement can be found in the relevant essays
   in Warren Hofstra (ed.), *Ulster to America: The Scots-Irish migration experience,
   1680–1730* (Knoxville, 2012).

6 Griffin, *People with no name*; Patrick Griffin, '"Irish" migration in the
   eighteenth century: or the strange case for the "Scots/Irish"' in James Kelly
   (ed.), *Cambridge history of Ireland: volume III, 1730–1880* (London, 2018).

7 Frank Thistelthwaite, 'Migration from Europe overseas in the nineteenth and
   twentieth centuries' in Comite International des Sciences Historiques, *XIe
   Congres International des Sciences Historiques, Rapports: V: Histoire
   contemporaine* (Stockholm, 1960), pp 32–60.

8 Stephen Brumwell, *Redcoats: the British soldier and war in the Americas,
   1755–1763* (New York, 2006).

9 T. H. Breen, 'An Irish revolution in eighteenth-century America', *Field Day
   Review*, 2 (2006), pp 275–82.

10 David N. Doyle, *Ireland, Irishmen, and revolutionary America, 1760–1820*
   (Cork, 1981).

11 David A. Wilson, *United Irishmen, United States: immigrant radicals in the
   early republic* (Ithaca, NY, 2011); see also Peter Gilmore, Trevor Parkhill and
   William Roulston, *Exiles of '98: Ulster Presbyterians and the United States*
   (Belfast, 2018).

Suggested further reading

The links between Ireland and America stretch back at least to the Middle Ages. However, the purposeful emigration which over centuries brought so many Irish-born across the Atlantic, began, as far as is known, with individuals travelling alone or in very small groups, in the last quarter of the seventeenth century. The exodus which was planned and organised in 1718, of families and even whole communities from north and north-west Ulster, marks a step-change in the story of emigration and also in American history; a number of the individuals featured in this volume were involved in these momentous events. Others made their contribution to American history in the early eighteenth century, a period which has not been as thoroughly researched as later eras. Awareness of the significance of Ireland in the Atlantic economy and in the colonial period has grown, both among historians and the general public, as the tercentenary in 2018 focused attention on the events of 1718.

The Dictionary of Irish Biography (DIB), published by the Royal Irish Academy and Cambridge University Press in hard copy in 2009 and online at that date and since, is the source of the material curated and edited in this volume. Many of the other articles in the DIB will prove invaluable for researchers and family historians interested in following up connections or understanding the Irish background, and of course the sources listed in notes to each of the articles published here will provide useful guidance on particularly important aspects of local and international history.

This bibliographical sketch will not concern itself with wider political, military and social histories of the period, but will look at works whose focus is specifically the links across the Atlantic and on the Atlantic world, the significance of which are highlighted in Patrick Griffin's Introduction to the present volume. One of Griffin's works can stand first in this review: *The people with no name: Ireland's Ulster Scots, America's Scots Irish and the creation of a British Atlantic world, 1689–1764* (Princeton, 2001). Kerby A. Miller, one of the scholars who first began to see the Atlantic as a bridge rather than a dividing ocean, summed up thirty years of work in *Ireland and Irish America. Culture, class and transatlantic migration* (Dublin, 2008). Earlier Miller wrote *Emigrants and exiles: Ireland and the Irish exodus to North America* (Oxford, 1985). With David N. Doyle, Bruce D. Boling and Arnold Schrier, he published *Irish immigrants in the land of Canaan: letters and memoirs from colonial and revolutionary America* (New York and Oxford, 2003). H. Tyler Blethen and Curtis W. Wood edited *Ulster and*

North America: transatlantic perspectives on the Scotch-Irish (Tuscaloosa, 1997), and Warren F. Hofstra edited a useful collection of essays, *Ulster to America: the Scots-Irish migration experience 1680–1830* (Knoxville, 2012), in which his introduction draws attention to the historiographic hinterland of the term 'Scots-Irish'.

Earlier works on the Scots-Irish or Scotch-Irish pay scant attention to the history of emigrants from other traditions and origins, but at least E. R. R. Green (ed.), *Essays in Scotch-Irish history* (Belfast, 1969), Charles A. Hanna, *The Scotch-Irish, or the Scot in North Britain, North Ireland and North America* (New York, 1902), and especially Charles K. Bolton, *Scotch-Irish pioneers in Ulster and America* (Boston, 1910) gave the term 'Scotch-Irish' a good deal more academic respectability than perhaps it had previously deserved. A work of great value was *Ulster emigration to colonial America, 1718–1775* (London, 1966), by R. J. Dickson (reprinted many times, and republished on its fiftieth anniversary in 2016 by the Ulster Historical Foundation with an important new introduction and updated perspectives on the subject by Patrick Fitzgerald).

Patrick Fitzgerald and Brian Lambkin provide a wider view of emigration and an authoritative summary in *Migration in Irish history, 1607–2007* (Basingstoke, 2008). During most of the period in which the lives analysed here were being lived, Canada as a separate entity had not yet been formed. However, in their book *Irish emigration and Canadian settlement: patterns, links and letters* (Toronto, 1990), Cecil J. Houston and William J. Smyth explored ways in which the northern part of 'British North America' experienced eighteenth-century events differently. Seventeenth- and eighteenth-century connections between Waterford, Munster and the northeastern shores of British America, the Atlantic Provinces of today, are explored in articles by John Mannion in *Newfoundland Studies*, especially in volume 17 (2001), and elsewhere, and in Brendan O'Grady, *Exiles and islanders: the Irish settlers of Prince Edward Island* (Montreal and Kingston, 2004).

A good number of articles and books by Louis M. Cullen draw attention to the relevance of transnational perspectives on economic history, as does Nicholas Canny, *Kingdom and colony: Ireland in the Atlantic world, 1560–1800* (Baltimore, 1988). Analysing trade patterns, Thomas M. Truxes published *Irish-American trade, 1660–1783* (Cambridge, 2004), and draws attention to the vital flaxseed trade. Richard K. MacMaster, *Scotch-Irish merchants in colonial America* (Belfast, 2009) concentrates on the mercantile elite, especially on their family networks that sustained trade in developing economies.

Religion, as always in Irish matters, must be acknowledged as a factor which both united and divided. David A. Wilson and Mark G. Spencer edited *Ulster Presbyterians in the Atlantic world: religion, politics and identity* (Dublin, 2006), and Rankin Sherling, *The invisible Irish: finding Protestants in the nineteenth-century migration to America* (Montreal and Kingston, 2016), despite the title, provides useful background material on eighteenth-century migration. The contribution of Catholics to colonial settlements and Atlantic networks has perhaps not been sufficiently explored; it is to be hoped that the essays in this volume will help to highlight this aspect of the shared histories.

The essays re-published here, by kind permission of Cambridge University Press, have been selected for their individual interest and significance in history, but also to serve as named representatives of so very many un-named people, who sadly left the land of their birth, who have been forgotten both there and in the New World, and who deserve to be acknowledged for their hardships, work and sacrifice.

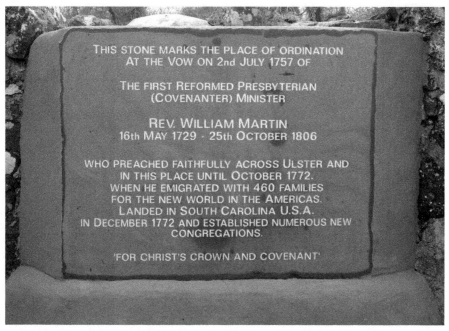

Memorial to Rev. William Martin, The Vow, Ballymoney, Co. Antrim

ILLUSTRATIONS

Francis Alison

An engraving by
John James Barralet

John Barry

George Berkeley

Anne Bonney (left)

Gravestone of William Boyd, Taughboyne, Co. Donegal

Sir Guy Carleton

Matthew Clerk

Sir Arthur Dobbs

Thomas Donegan

Philip Embury's church, New York

John Dunlap

Samuel Finley

Thomas Fitzsimons

Hugh Gaine

Barbara Heck

Charles Inglis

William Irvine

Guy Johnson

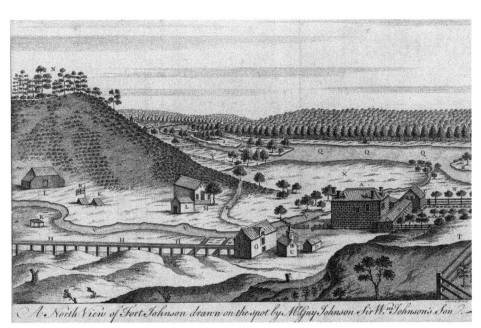

Drawing of Fort Johnson by Guy Johnson

Sir William Johnson

John Johnston

John Johnston's House in Sault Ste Marie

James Logan

Matthew Lyon

Painting by Henry Alexander Ogden,
'Francis Makemie's trial before Lord Cornbury'

James McHenry

James MacSparran

Richard Montgomery

William Paterson

William Penn

James Smith

George Taylor

Gilbert Tennent

Charles Thomson

Matthew Thornton

Hugh Waddell

Sir Peter Warren

THE BIOGRAPHIES

Alison, Francis
1705–79
Presbyterian minister and educator

Francis Alison was born in the parish of Leck, Co. Donegal, son of Robert Alison, weaver, who may have been fairly well off, and who seems to have died in 1725; Francis's mother's name is unknown, but her first name was possibly Mary. There is said to have been at least one other son; Alison is known to have had at least one sister, whose son James Latta was born in Donegal (1732), and who also became a prominent Presbyterian minister and schoolteacher in Pennsylvania.

Alison received an excellent grounding in Latin, Greek, and other subjects, probably from a local minister or at Raphoe Royal School close to his home, before he graduated MA (1733) from the University of Edinburgh. It is possible that he studied divinity in Glasgow University for two years after 1733, and would have been taught there by the Ulster-born philosopher, Francis Hutcheson. Alison knew Hutcheson well enough to write to him (1744) from America, seeking his advice on suitable textbooks and curricula. Hutcheson's teaching was of great importance in the development of what historians have labelled 'the Scottish Enlightenment'. The Scottish universities were among the most distinguished educational institutions in Europe at the time, in the forefront of new developments in thought and practice.

In June 1735 Alison was licensed by the presbytery of Letterkenny to preach, and with other family members left Ireland for America. He was possibly a private tutor in Maryland for a time, and a ministerial probationer in the New Castle presbytery, before being ordained (1737) as minister of New London Presbyterian church in Chester county, Pennsylvania. He spent fifteen years there, well regarded by his congregation and increasingly renowned as a champion of the 'Old Side' of Presbyterianism. Ministers who held to the 'Old Side' believed that the church should have an educated ministry, formed within the traditional patterns of academic training and collegial examination. They also valued decorum in worship, in contrast to the 'New Side', inspired by men such as William and Gilbert Tennent, who stressed the importance of enthusiasm, emotion, and conversion experience in religious life. In the late 1730s the division in American Presbyterianism became overt when 'New Side' supporters walked out of a synod meeting that called for the establishment by church authorities of a traditional style of academy to train ministers; and the break became complete in 1741 when a new synod was set up to hold the ministers and congregations who were participants in the 'Great Awakening'. Alison published a pamphlet setting out the antagonism of the 'Old Side' ministers to Gilbert Tennent's often exasperating claims and

2

activities. In 1758 Alison was instrumental in bringing about a reunification of the two synods, though discord continued for many years thereafter.

Alison lamented the dearth of educational opportunities in the colonies, and was concerned that the frontier life was inimical to intellectual culture. By 1743 (and possibly as early as 1739) he had established a grammar school in his home in New London, which was immediately successful, and in which he and assistants taught not only the learned languages to the highest standard, but also English grammar, philosophy, *belles lettres*, and natural philosophy, including mathematics. The school expanded into separate premises, and was very soon adopted as its official academy by the presbytery of Philadelphia, which also provided financial support. Because of this support the school provided free education, but not just for Presbyterians; it was open to all denominations. Alison was credited with 'first and most effectually' enlightening the middle colonies in both 'useful and ornamental learning' (Matthew Wilson, quoted in *The University of Delaware: a history*). He was the first colonial educator whose curriculum and methods reveal the influence of the principles of the Scottish Enlightenment; principles which historians of ideas describe as seminal in various aspects of American history and politics. Alison's first class was a remarkable group of young men, almost all of Scots-Irish birth or descent, and many later notable in the American independence movement and in the new republic; they included Charles Thomson, later secretary to the Continental Congress, and Alison's nephew James Latta. In the course of his career Alison taught, and presumably inspired, five signers of the Declaration of Independence, including James Smith (d. 1806), several state governors, four generals in the Continental army, fifteen congressmen, and two chaplains to Congress, as well as notable doctors, ministers, and scholars.

In 1752 Alison moved to Philadelphia to be one of the two ministers of the First Presbyterian congregation there, and was rector and master of the Latin school in the Academy of Philadelphia, established a few years earlier. The Academy expanded rapidly, and in 1755 became known as the College of Philadelphia, and after 1779 as the University of Pennsylvania. Alison remained there as a professor and as vice-provost of the college until his death, recognised by contemporaries as the 'greatest classical scholar in America' (*ANB*).

Alison's influence on American education extended well beyond his own lifetime. He was able to adapt to the new way of life and the resulting demand for practical instruction, while still focusing on the subjects of traditional scholarship. His example 'spread [a love of learning] through the new world and founded all the schools and academies round' (*University of Delaware: a history*). His academy in New London, after several moves and different masters, was backed by 'Old Side' ministers in opposition to the 'New Side' College of New Jersey in Princeton, and eventually became a chartered body in 1767 as Newark Academy, with Francis Alison as president of the board of trustees. Ultimately, despite vicissitudes during the War of Independence, it became the University of Delaware. For his services to education, Alison received honorary degrees from Yale and Princeton and an honorary doctorate of divinity from Glasgow (1756).

Alison's influence on American political thought, and ultimately on American history, extended well beyond a schoolmaster's direct impact on his pupils. He was a leading figure from the early 1760s in moves to consolidate Scots-Irish Presbyterian opinion against what he regarded as dangerous initiatives from the English government and the authorities in the colony of Pennsylvania; he was worried about threatened legislation which would restrict colonial trade, and he led Presbyterian clergy in opposition to the Stamp Act of 1765 and the Townshend Acts of 1767. He was especially alarmed by the possibility that the Anglican church would in time become the established church in America, with the introduction of bishops in American sees. This prospect was anathema to someone of Alison's background; Ulster Presbyterians had no desire to live again under what they castigated as episcopal tyranny.

Alison and two collaborators published essays under the title of 'The Centinel' in the *Pennsylvania Journal* in the spring of 1768; in these, Alison's hand is most clearly evident, and his forceful arguments against established churches and the threats to civil and religious liberty in the colonies were very effective. At the same time he made contact to establish common cause with leaders of the New England congregational churches, and with Dissenters of German origin; annual meetings, called 'general conventions', took place between 1767 and 1775, and are credited with having helped to form a ground swell of radical opinion in the colonies which ultimately led to the break with England. Alison in a private letter in 1768 expressed his hope that 'sons of liberty' in America would unite to combat the threat of an established church and attendant evils (Miller, 518). Kerby Miller comments that Alison, 'perhaps more than any other public figure, helped prepare Pennsylvania's Scots-Irish for their prominent role in the American revolution' (ibid., 510).

Alison's other contributions to public life were of considerable importance. In his own assessment of his career, he believed that his efforts for the welfare of ministers and their dependents were as important as his stand against what he believed were the dangerous excesses of the religious innovations of the 'Great Awakening'. With the help of subscriptions from Presbyterians in Britain and Ireland and locally, Alison established the Presbyterian Ministers' Fund, a mutual assistance institution incorporated in 1759, on a Scottish model. It is said to have been the first life insurance company in America, predating others by eighty years. The fund loaned money to the Continental Congress to help finance the War of Independence. Its name was changed in 1994 when it was amalgamated with another company, but its headquarters, called the Alison Building in honour of the founder, remained a landmark in downtown Philadelphia.

Shortly after his ordination in New London, Alison married (1737) Hannah (b. 1715 in Yorkshire, England), daughter of James Armitage, a prominent citizen of New Castle, Delaware. Hannah's younger half-sister, Sara Armitage, married Thomas McKean (1734–1817) who had been educated by Alison. McKean's parents were Presbyterians from Ballymoney in the north of Ireland, who had emigrated in 1718 to a settlement that became Londonderry, New Hampshire. He was one of the most influential officeholders and politicians of the revolutionary period, a signer of the Declaration of Independence. Francis and Hannah Alison had two daughters and four sons. Two of the sons died in infancy, and another died unmarried in 1781. Alison did not live to see the outcome of the colonists' struggle for independence; he died 28 November 1779 in Philadelphia, at the height of the war.

Linde Lunney

SOURCES
Leonard Allison Morrison, *The history of the Allison or Alison family in Europe and America, AD 1135 to 1892* (1893), 127–8; Guy Souilliard Klett, *Presbyterians in colonial Pennsylvania* (1937); Elizabeth Nybakken, 'In the Irish tradition: pre-revolutionary academies in America', *History of Education Quarterly*, xxxvii, no. 2 (1997), 163–83; Amy Worden, 'Presbyterians suing for colonial-era contributions' (9 Dec. 1998) online at www.pcusa.org/pcnews/oldnews/1998/98408.htm; *ANB* on Francis Alison and Thomas McKean; Kerby A. Miller, *Irish immigrants in the land of Canaan: letters and memoirs from colonial and revolutionary America* (2003), passim, but especially 510–21; 'Donegal will index', transcribed by Cathy Joint Labath, online at www.ulsterancestry.com; 'James Latta (1732–1801)', online at http://archives.upenn.edu/histy/features/1700s/people/latta_james.html; 'The University of Delaware: a history', and Carol Hoffecker, 'The story of the Rev. Dr Francis Alison', online on University of Delaware website, www.udel.edu (internet material accessed Dec. 2007)

Barralet, John James
c. 1747–1815
Artist and drawing master

John James Barralet was born in Dublin, son of a Huguenot émigré. He is known to have at least two brothers, one of whom, John Melchior Barralet (*c.* 1750–*c.* 1787), also became an artist, practising mainly in London.

Barralet received his artistic training at two of the Dublin Society's drawing schools, where he studied under Robert Lucius West and James Mannin. He was evidently a talented pupil, as he was awarded two premiums for 'Drawing of human figures and heads' and 'Inventions of designs and patterns' in 1764, and a third for 'Original design in patterns' in 1766 (Raley, 19). Having completed his studies, he worked as an artist in Dublin, becoming known as a gifted drawing teacher. He later moved to London, though the exact date of his departure for London is uncertain – dates alternating between 1766 and 1770, when his name appears among the signatories of the 'Rolls of declaration' supporting the Incorporated Society of Artists. He made his mark in London's artistic circles, exhibiting topographical landscapes and subject pieces at the Royal Academy (1770–76), the Society of Arts (who awarded him a golden palette for his 'View of Brentford from Kew' in 1774), and the Society of Artists (1773–80), who elected him a fellow and director in 1777. In that year he submitted six landscapes to the exhibition in the great room at the Royal Exchange, Strand. Throughout this period Barralet continued to teach, establishing drawing-schools in James's Street, Golden Square (1773), and St Alban's Street, Pall Mall (1777). He was among the group of artists who pioneered the production of small full-length watercolour portraits on paper.

In 1779 he returned to Dublin and, on the recommendation of Mannin, then critically ill, was appointed as his temporary replacement at the Dublin Society's School for Ornament Drawing. He remained in this post after Mannin's death in June 1779. However, despite his friendship with two speakers of the Irish House of Commons, John Foster and Edmund Sexton Pery, both vice-presidents of the society, and his popularity among staff and pupils at the school, Barralet was defeated in the November 1779 election for the mastership by William Waldron, a protégé of the 2nd duke of Leinster. Waldron subsequently proved an unsatisfactory teacher. When receiving his final payment from the society, Barralet was awarded a gratuity of £45 'in consideration of his great merit as an artist; and his diligence and attention in superintending the said school' (Turpin, 46).

Remaining in Dublin, Barralet lived at various times in George's Court, South Cumberland Road, and Ballsbridge. In 1780 he accompanied the Huguenot artist Gabriel Beranger on a sketching tour of Wicklow and Wexford. Twenty-three of his drawings were later engraved for inclusion in Francis Grose's *Antiquities of Ireland* (1791–5). His illustrations also appeared in Thomas Milton's *Views of the seats in Ireland* (1783–93), and his designs for allegorical cartouches were included in Alexander Taylor's *New map of Ireland* (1793).

Barralet continued to exhibit, submitting paintings to the Society of Artists Exhibition in William Street (1780), while supplementing his income through work as a scene-painter in the Crow Street Theatre (1782), and with the glass-staining firm of Richard Hand and Thomas Chebsey. His friendship with John Foster paid dividends in 1786 when Foster commissioned him to paint his family on the steps of their newly built country home at Oriel Temple, Co. Louth. He subsequently spent some time working in Glenarm, Co. Antrim, where he was employed as a drawing-master to the family of Randal MacDonnell, 6th earl of Antrim. During his stay there in the late 1780s he also executed a number of landscapes.

Unable to make an adequate living in Ireland, Barralet emigrated to America, settling in Philadelphia, where in December 1794 he helped establish the short-lived 'Associate Artists of Philadelphia'. He soon found Philadelphians had little interest in painting, and as a result worked primarily as an illustrator and engraver. Among his most popular pieces were his engravings of George Washington, the first of which was advertised in April 1795. It was followed by another series of prints in 1799, and in 1802 by his best-known work, 'The apotheosis of Washington'. Produced to mark the president's death, the print remained in circulation for some years, and after the assassination in 1865 of Abraham Lincoln inspired similar popular prints. He also designed the membership certificate for the local Hibernian Society (1798). Among the significant commissions Barralet received in Philadelphia were those for paintings of the Market Street Bridge and the house of the publisher John Dunlap, the latter being completed after 1806. In 1811 Barralet was appointed professor of drawing from the antique at the Academy of Art in Philadelphia. He is thought to have invented a ruling machine for engravers and improved the ink used for copperplate prints. Described by his American friends as 'a man of talent without discretion or anything like common prudence; prodigally generous, and graspingly poor' (Rayley, 19), in later years he became renowned for his eccentric manner and untidy appearance. After several years of poor health he died in poverty (16 January 1815) in Philadelphia. He married twice. He left his first wife and a son and daughter in Ireland, and had two sons by his second wife, who predeceased him.

Frances Clarke

SOURCES
Walter G. Strickland, *A dictionary of Irish artists* (2 vols, 1913, repr. 1969); Anne Crookshank and the Knight of Glin, *The painters of Ireland c. 1660–1920* (1978); id., *Ireland's painters* (2002); Robert L. Raley, 'John James Barralet in Dublin and Philadelphia', *Irish Arts Review*, ii, no. 3 (autumn 1985), 19–25; Patricia Butler, *Three hundred years of Irish watercolours and drawings* (1990); John Turpin, *A school of art in Dublin since the eighteenth century* (1995); Nicola Figgis, 'Barralet, John James', *Irish art and architecture*, 2 (2014)

Barry, John
1745–1803
United States Navy captain

John Barry was born in Ballysampson, Tacumshane parish, Co. Wexford, son of John Barry, clerk and small farmer, and Catherine Barry (née Kelly). He went to sea in 1755 and settled in Philadelphia in 1760. He continued to work as a merchant sailor and became a ship's master in 1766.

On the outbreak of the revolutionary war he relinquished command of his ship, the *Black Prince*, which was renamed as the *Alfred* and became the first ship in the Continental navy. Barry helped prepare this ship for naval service and when he offered his own services to Congress, he was commissioned as a captain in the Continental navy on 14 March 1776. He took command of the *Lexington* and on 6 April 1776 captured HMS *Edward* after a running fight lasting an hour. This was the first occasion on which a regularly commissioned American ship made a capture. After capturing two other British sloops, he was given command of the *Effingham*, a modern frigate then being built in Philadelphia. Due to the British blockade the ship never actually went to sea and was burned by British forces in 1777. Spending much of the next two years serving in the army, he commanded an artillery battery formed using the crew and guns from the *Effingham* and fought at the battles of Trenton (1776) and Princeton (1777). Later that year he led four small boats into Delaware Bay and cut out and captured an armed schooner and several transports filled with supplies. In March 1778 he received a note of thanks from George Washington for this exploit.

On 25 September 1778 he set out from Boston in the *Raleigh* but was immediately sighted by HMS *Experiment* and HMS *Unicorn*. After a long chase that lasted several days, he engaged the British ships in an unequal fight before running his ship aground on Wooden Ball Island near Penobscot Bay, saving the lives of most of his crew. The resulting court martial found no fault in his conduct despite the fact that the *Raleigh* was later refloated by a British boarding party and used by the Royal Navy.

As there was no prospect of a new command he made commercial voyages to the West Indies (1779–80). In early 1781 he was given command of the *Alliance*, which was then the most powerful ship in the Continental navy. This marked the beginning of a more successful phase of his career, and in February 1781 he sailed for France, carrying Col. John Laurens and Thomas Paine. During the return voyage he captured two privateers and two merchant vessels. After an obstinate fight on 23 May 1781 he captured the sloops HMS *Atlanta* and HMS *Trepassy*. He was badly wounded by grapeshot in the left shoulder during this action and received a formal vote of thanks from Congress in June 1781. In March

1782 he escorted a much-needed convoy of gold from Cuba, and on a cruise in August he captured nine transport ships sailing out of Jamaica. He fought the last naval action of the war when (10 March 1783) he attacked HMS *Sybil* off Cape Canaveral. After the end of the war, he championed the cause of ex-sailors, securing them pension rights from Congress. He was also politically active, lobbying congressmen in an effort to promote a federal system of government.

As master of the merchant ship *Asia* he made a profitable trip to China between December 1787 and June 1789. On the foundation of the United States Navy in June 1794, he was listed as the senior captain of the new service. He bore the courtesy title of 'commodore' for the remainder of his career, the rank not existing officially until 1862. He oversaw the construction of a new frigate, the *United States*, and then commanded this ship in the West Indies during the quasi-French-American war (1797–1801). He enjoyed a successful campaign against privateers and French naval vessels in the West Indies. On 3 February 1799 he took part in the last naval action of the war when he captured the *L'amour de la patrie* off Martinique. He later carried treaty negotiators to France in December 1799 and then commanded the Guadeloupe station until the end of the war.

Throughout his life he suffered from asthma and his health went into a further decline in 1803. He died on 13 September 1803 at Strawberry Hill, Philadelphia, and was buried in St Mary's Roman Catholic churchyard. He is often referred to as the 'father of the American navy' as his career was inextricably linked with the early development of the USN. He trained many officers who were later to have distinguished careers in the Barbary wars and the War of 1812. These included James Barron, Stephen Decatur, and Charles Stewart, who were known as 'Barry's boys'. Many of his ideas on naval organisation and training were retained in the new service.

He married first (1767) Mary Clary or Cleary of Philadelphia. After her death in 1774, he married Sarah Austin (d. *c.* 1803) in 1777. There were no children from either marriage. There are statues of Barry in Independence Square, Philadelphia, in Lafayette Square, Washington, DC, and in Crescent Quay, Wexford. The Wexford statue was presented to the town in 1956 by President Dwight D. Eisenhower. In 1981 President Ronald Reagan designated 13 September as 'Commodore John Barry Day'.

There are collections of Barry papers in the Barnes collection of the Naval History Society of New York and in the Maritime Museum Library, Philadelphia. To date, four different USN ships have borne the name USS *Barry*.

David Murphy

SOURCES
Webb; *DNB*; *Studies: an Irish Quarterly Review*, xxiv (1934), 623–33; W. B. Clark, *Gallant John Barry* (1938); *DAB*; F. E. Benz, *Commodore Barry, naval hero* (1950); *Irish Sword*, ii, no. 8 (1956), 249–56; *Capuchin Annual 1957*, 409–14; L. Wibberley, *John Barry, father of the navy* (1957); *Journal of the Old Wexford Society*, i (1968), 30–32; *ADB*; Bernard Browne, *County Wexford connections* (1985), 7; Richard Humble, *History of the United States Navy* (1988)

Berkeley, George
1685–1753
Philosopher and Church of Ireland bishop of Cloyne

George Berkeley was born on 12 March 1685 in or near Kilkenny city, and spent his childhood at Dysart Castle, Thomastown, Co. Kilkenny. Little is known of his parents other than that his father, William Berkeley, came to Ireland from Staffordshire, and that his mother may have been Elisabeth Southerne, daughter of a Dublin brewer and a descendant through her maternal line of Archbishop James Ussher. Though often subsequently described as one of the great British empiricist philosophers, George robustly affirmed his own Irishness in his writings. He was the eldest of six brothers; the others in order of age were Rowland, Ralph, William, Robert, and Thomas.

EDUCATION AND EARLY CAREER
Berkeley entered Kilkenny College (also the school of Jonathan Swift and the dramatist William Congreve) on 17 July 1696, placed in the second highest class on entry. He entered Trinity College Dublin (TCD) on 21 March 1700. There he was influenced by a thriving intellectual group of fellow-students and tutors. Berkeley studied maths, logic, philosophy, Greek, Latin, French, and Hebrew. John Locke's *Essay concerning human understanding* (1690) was a central part of the philosophy course, introduced to the curriculum by Locke's friend William Molyneux within two years of publication. Berkeley received his BA degree on 24 February 1704. As was customary for students of distinction, he stayed in college after graduating to study for a fellowship, which was to be achieved after a competitive examination for a very limited number of places. Fellows were obliged to take holy orders and abstain from marriage during their tenure. He became a fellow in June 1707 and subsequently held a number of college offices including librarian (1709), junior dean (1710), junior Greek lecturer (1712), senior Greek lecturer (1721), divinity lecturer and preacher (1721), senior proctor (1722), and Hebrew lecturer (1723), before relinquishing his fellowship on 18 May 1724. He was ordained priest in the

Church of Ireland by St George Ashe, bishop of Clogher and former provost of Trinity, in spring 1710, which led to a controversy with William King, archbishop of Dublin, whose permission had not been sought for the ordination of Berkeley by another bishop in his diocese. This perceived affront led to King prosecuting Berkeley in the diocesan court and to Berkeley writing an apology. In form, this was a trial of jurisdiction between TCD and the archbishop of Dublin – but Berkeley and King had also differed on political and theological issues. Berkeley was a tory, King a whig who was present when Berkeley preached the sermon articulating tory doctrine that was to become *Passive obedience* (1712). Having such a powerful adversary would influence Berkeley's quest for preferment in the Church of Ireland, depending as it did primarily on the grace and favour of powerful elements in that church.

PHILOSOPHICAL IDEALISM: *A TREATISE* AND *THREE DIALOGUES*

Berkeley's career can be divided into three phases, usefully labelled by David Berman as 'philosophical idealism', 'social idealism', and 'medical idealism' respectively. In the first he develops a unique philosophical system, in the second he is one of the foremost influences on American education, and in the third he reveals himself as a kindly and humane pastor, concerned with the practical and spiritual concerns of the people for whom he was responsible. His philosophical fame rests primarily on three books published between 1709 and 1713. In the first, *An essay towards a new theory of vision* (Dublin, 1709), he developed an account of vision that would later support his more famous immaterialist hypothesis. The philosophical problems raised by Locke and Molyneux required an accurate account of vision, and vision is often appealed to by those who want to defend the existence of mind-independent matter: they maintain you just *see* it. In the *Essay* Berkeley investigated the nature of the object perceived, distinguishing between what is immediately perceived and what is subsequently inferred. He also distinguished sharply between objects yielded by the sense modality of sight and those yielded by touch. However, he did not as yet expound the view with which he is most associated – immaterialism.

A treatise concerning the principles of human knowledge (Dublin, 1710) is Berkeley's masterpiece. In it he articulates and defends the full-blown philosophy of immaterialism. This doctrine, also known as subjective idealism, denies the existence of matter and goes on to argue that the very idea of matter is nonsensical. The view was as startling and counterintuitive in Berkeley's time as it is now. However, his greatness lies in the power and subtlety of the arguments that lead to this conclusion. The introduction deals with the doctrine of abstract ideas, which claims that there are special kinds of ideas that refer to universal general concepts (e.g. the abstract idea of 'dog' in general rather than of this or that specific dog). Berkeley rejects this claim, arguing that all ideas are of individuals, that the purported general ideas do not exist, and that we refer to general features of reality using only individual ideas (e.g. we use the idea of a specific dog, with specific qualities, to stand for dogs in general). The rejected doctrine had been extensively used in scholastic thought and by those supporting the view that matter exists. In the body of the *Principles* Berkeley uses the rejection of abstract ideas to argue against the existence of matter. He begins the main text with the account of mind and knowledge that was accepted by most of his contemporaries, and shows how it led inevitably to idealistic conclusions. What are known immediately are ideas. Some ideas come from sources other than the mind; they are not under the control of the will. Others are the products of memory or imagination and can be summoned up at will. There are therefore two kinds of thing whose existence is certain: ideas and minds. Ideas have no power in themselves to cause anything else, whereas minds have causal powers. According to Berkeley, the truth of all this can be verified through introspection. He then notes that there is a strange doctrine that asserts that there is such a thing as matter which is totally independent of minds and ideas. It is important to note that the doctrine of matter that Berkeley rejects is a metaphysical doctrine: it holds that the fundamental nature of reality is such that there exist things that have no relationship whatsoever to any mind whatsoever. It is not the commonsense doctrine that there exist tables and chairs and rocks in the world; rather, it is a more subtle doctrine about how to interpret the reality of such commonsense objects. The materialist argues that these things can exist without any mind whatsoever thinking of them. Berkeley rejects that view. However, he is not claiming that the world depends on human minds for its existence; rather, he holds the view that reality consists of ideas in the mind of God. What is perceived as reality is constituted by ideas directly produced by the will of God. Human minds perceive these ideas and in so doing understand the world. It makes no sense to talk of inert matter existing independently of God's mind.

Berkeley's arguments against the metaphysical notion of matter are of most importance to philosophers. He trenchantly criticised the various moves the materialist might make to uphold such a position, and furthermore showed how his position refuted scepticism, upheld religion, explained scientific knowledge, and produced a coherent picture of reality, all resting on what were regarded as indisputable premises about the nature of thought and the mind. However, the wits of Dublin and London were quick to pick on the apparently absurd aspect of Berkeley's doctrine; various negative opinions were offered as to his state of sanity, his seriousness, and his presumptuousness. Despite his patient attempts to convince opponents on dialectical points, the entire literary establishment ridiculed the young

Irishman's bizarre views. Just as Hume's subsequent *magnum opus* was disappointingly received, 'falling deadborn from the press' (David Fate Norton (ed.), *The Cambridge companion to Hume* (1993), app. II, 352), Berkeley's was met with waves of mirth and witticism at its author's expense. Discouraging as this might be to such a sober author, he set to presenting his ideas in a form that would convince the intellectual leaders of his day. The result was his second great work, *The three dialogues between Hylas and Philonous* (London, 1713). As much a work of literature as philosophy, it set out to defend immaterialism in a way compelling to its readers. Philonous is the proponent of Berkeley's position, while Hylas defends the materialist position. The detailed accounts of the *Principles* are left out, but certain issues are treated in greater detail; for example, the discussion of the relativity of perception to the perceiver.

This time Berkeley's work took London by storm. He was fêted by Pope, Swift, Addison, and Steele, visited court, dined at Oxford, and had coffee with the wits. Contacts were forged at this period that would bear fruit in later stages of his career, especially in connection with preferment in the Church of Ireland and funding his Bermuda project. A final piece of writing from this period is worth noting: *Passive obedience* (Dublin, 1712), a pamphlet consisting of three sermons delivered in TCD chapel. It deals with the question of what sort of allegiance is due to government, and in what circumstances – a burning question only two decades after the Glorious Revolution and just before renewed Jacobite unrest. Berkeley trod a delicate line between supporting the revolution that led to the Williamite regime, and opposing Jacobite claims of the justice of displacing it in turn. He argued the tory doctrine that revolution is allowable only *in extremis* and that the Jacobites could not establish that such circumstances prevailed; hence the *de facto* government is owed passive obedience.

THE CONTINENT, AMERICA, AND SOCIAL IDEALISM

The period 1713–35 contrasted with both the preceding and subsequent periods in Berkeley's career in the activism he displayed and the travel he undertook. First, he engaged in two tours of Italy: October 1713–August 1714 and autumn 1716–autumn 1720. During this time he still held his fellowship at TCD, but absence due to travel explains the nine-year gap between being junior and senior Greek lecturer. On the first tour he was secretary and chaplain to Lord Peterborough, ambassador to the king of Sicily. As he passed through France, it seems likely that he met with the philosopher Malebranche in Paris. He left Peterborough's group, its mission accomplished, in June 1714 and returned to London. Writing to his friend Percival on complaints about his absence from college, he wondered why he should be singled out, given the number of fellows absent and he the only one with royal authority for it! The second tour was as tutor to the bishop of Clogher's son, George Ashe, an agreeable but sickly travelling companion. During these four years, Berkeley developed a love for painting and architecture. His admiration of Italian art was not uncritical: he observed that the ancients had indifferent statuaries as well as the moderns. He attended religious ceremonies in Rome with, as he noted, fine singing, much incensing and carrying about with dressing and undressing of the pope. He visited Naples, Sicily, Florence, and planned to travel home in 1719, but delayed until August 1720 for unknown reasons – possibly the health of his companion. In that year he wrote a treatise called *De motu* for a competition on motion organised by the Académie Royal des Science in Paris. It did not win, but was published the following year in London. In it he developed in greater detail the criticisms of Newtonian science adumbrated in the *Principles*. Twentieth-century philosophers of science have seen anticipations of modern instrumentalist theories of science in it. The other literary event of note during this Italian sojourn was his losing the manuscript of the planned second part of the *Principles*. He never rewrote it, and it has never been recovered.

On his return to Ireland in 1721, Berkeley resumed duties at TCD, but as was normal for one in his position he began to seek preferment in the Church of Ireland. As a senior fellow he earned about £80 a year, sufficient to keep him in continual debt to the college. During this time he conceived the idea of establishing a college in the American colonies, where sons of the planters and Native Americans would be educated to MA standard. In 1724 Berkeley became dean of Derry and severed his connection with Trinity. The deanship was worth £1,250 a year, and it was normal for the incumbent to be an absentee with curates in his stead. Such financial security allowed Berkeley to pursue his project with renewed vigour. He raised subscriptions, acquired pledges from fellows of Trinity to accompany him, and gained a royal charter for the college and a promise from the British parliament of a grant of £20,000. The college, called St Paul's, would be founded in the Bermudas, a location chosen because he believed it was equidistant from all the other colonies, with fertile soil and fair climate. He sailed for America in September 1728. Just before he left, he married Anne, daughter of John Forster (1667–1720), MP for Dublin city (1703–14) and chief justice of the common pleas (1714–20). She accompanied Berkeley on the voyage with three others, the most notable of these being John Smibert, a portrait painter.

They arrived in Newport, Rhode Island, on 23 January 1729. Berkeley had decided not to go directly to Bermuda, and it is possible that he had begun to have doubts about the proposed location of the college even at that stage. (Maps were not very reliable and he had not realised that his 'ideal location' was in actuality some 600 miles from the mainland). He bought a farm in Middletown, Rhode Island, and waited there for the parliamentary grant for his college to come through. In the meantime he preached at Trinity church in Newport and made contact with Samuel Johnson, who was to become president of King's College, New York (subsequently Columbia University). Johnson's letters provide acute commentary on Berkeley's thought. Two children were born to George and Anne in Newport: Henry and Lucia, the latter of whom died and is buried in the grounds of Trinity church. While at his farm, Whitehall (since preserved as a Berkeley museum), he wrote *Alciphron, or The minute philosopher* (London, 1732), a defence of Christianity against atheists and free-thinkers, written in seven dialogues. By 1731 it had become clear that the Bermuda project was impracticable, and funding was consequently withheld by parliament. Berkeley returned to Europe. However, even though St Paul's, Bermuda, was never established, Berkeley had made an impact on American higher education. He was the foremost European intellectual of his era to visit the colonies. Johnson was to found King's College on principles expressed by Berkeley to him in correspondence. Berkeley gave collections of books to Yale and Harvard, and his farm was also granted to Yale, which named its divinity school after him. The state of California was subsequently to establish its university in a town named after George Berkeley.

BISHOP OF CLOYNE: MEDICAL IDEALISM AND SOCIAL CONCERN

Berkeley and his family waited in London (1731–4) while he sought ecclesiastical advancement from the royal court. It finally came (January 1734) in the form of the bishopric of Cloyne. In the meantime he had published *Alciphron*. He followed its line of argument again in the *Analyst* (London, 1734), defending Christian mysteries against free-thinkers. He argued that certain mathematical doctrines, accepted by the leading mathematicians of the time, were as mysterious as anything articulated in Christian doctrine. He engaged in controversy with various printed objections to his views in *A defence of free-thinking in mathematics* (London, 1735). This was to be his last book dealing with purely speculative issues. His subsequent writings reflected the practical concerns of a bishop in a poor, rural, Irish diocese.

Berkeley regarded his task in Cloyne as both spiritual and practical. He fulfilled the standard episcopal duties, including directing his clergy to use the Irish language when possible and appropriate. However, the temporal vicissitudes of his people exercised much of his time and occasioned his forays into print. Rural Ireland was grindingly poor. Berkeley's reflections on the economic situation led him to advocate self-sufficiency, and to attempt to rouse the poor from their passive acceptance of poverty, while chastising the powerful for allowing such a state. He presented his views on the economy, the theory of money, banking, and credit in the *Querist*, published anonymously in three parts (1735–7) and subsequently in abridged form over his name (1750). He encouraged local producers in Cloyne, establishing a spinning-school and a workhouse for vagrants, introducing the culture of flax and hemp, and himself wearing only home-produced products. In the severe winter of 1739–40 and the famine that followed, he distributed £20 among the poor of Cloyne every Monday until the next crops could be gathered. Widespread sickness following the famine led to his investigations of the medicinal powers of tar-water. In a situation where no medical infrastructure whatsoever existed for most of the population and infant mortality was extremely prevalent, he advocated this substance as a cure. Inspired by reports of its usage by Native Americans during his Bermuda expedition, he produced a treatise, *Siris* (1744), extolling its virtues. Sales of the reported panacea were enormous, once again provoking mirth at his expense by wits sceptical of the whole enterprise. However, his claims for the substance were modest; he found it good for alleviating his own health problems, and noted that others reported similar results. Berkeley was moved to take some form of action in the face of widespread ill health in Ireland. In his own family, enjoying a standard of living far above most people, the infant mortality rate was high. His Newport-born son Henry lived in Cloyne, along with George, born in London in 1733. Of the four children born in Cloyne, John and Sarah died in infancy, William died at fifteen in 1751, and it seems likely that his daughter Julia did not long survive her father.

As well as his social activism, his treatise-writing, and his voluminous correspondence with friends, British and American contacts, and fellow churchmen, Berkeley enjoyed a cultured existence at Cloyne. Many visitors sought him out. He regularly held concerts at his house, often as an alternative to card-playing, which he despised. A famous Italian virtuoso, Pasquilino, spent four years at his house as music tutor and concert giver at £200 a year. The house was adorned with paintings, including a Rubens and a Van Dyck.

DEATH AND LEGACY

Berkeley had personally supervised the tuition of his children in Cloyne. Henry had gone to France due to ill health. His son George went to Christ Church, Oxford, in 1752 and began to spend large sums of money. Berkeley travelled to Oxford to supervise his son's education, taking a house in Holywell Street. There his ill health intensified (he had long complained of an ulcer on his kidney), and he died on 14 January 1753. George subsequently pursued a career in the Church of England, becoming a canon of Canterbury. Berkeley was buried in Christ Church cathedral, Oxford, where a large monument in the nave commemorates him, appropriately enough close to a plaque commemorating John Locke, who is buried nearby. Contemporary portraits of Berkeley are in TCD; Yale; the National Portrait Gallery, London; and the National Gallery of Ireland.

Berkeley is unarguably Ireland's greatest philosopher, and his work is part of every standard undergraduate philosophy curriculum. It directly influenced Hume, Kant, and the positivists, and indirectly many more. However, his contribution to theology, mathematics, economics, and education has also been great. His ideas on national identity and self-sufficiency struck a chord with those otherwise so widely separated as William Butler Yeats and Éamon de Valera. A less tangible but no less real aspect of the man is the respect and love he generated among those who knew him. Pope ascribed to him 'ev'ry virtue under heav'n' in a famous quatrain. Swift, Johnson, Percival, Prior and many others showed their regard for him in their letters. His widow Anne wrote a fine account of his character to their son George after the bishop's death. Perhaps the best summing up of Berkeley's life and thought is in the words of the great Berkeley scholar Arthur Aston Luce, who remarked that one initially thinks on reading Berkeley that Berkeley is building a house, but subsequently discovers that he has built a church.

Paul O'Grady

SOURCES
D. Berman, *George Berkeley: idealism and the man* (1994); R. Houghton, D. Berman and M. Lapan, *Images of Berkeley* (1986); A. A. Luce, *The life of George Berkeley* (1949, repr. 1992); A. A. Luce and T. E. Jessop (ed.), *The works of George Berkeley* (9 vols, 1948–57)

Bonney, Anne
d. 1782
Pirate

Anne Bonney (or Bonny) was born in Co. Cork, the illegitimate daughter of William Cormac, a wealthy Cork lawyer or merchant, and his maidservant. According to Daniel Defoe, her first biographer, she was disguised as a boy during early childhood in order to conceal her identity. Later, to avoid local censure, Cormac took his mistress and child to South Carolina where, prospering as a merchant, he acquired a substantial plantation. Anne grew up in the colonies as an independent and strong-willed young woman, reputed to have stabbed her English maid with a case knife.

In 1718, when she married a poor seaman, James Bonney, her father turned her out of the house and the couple moved to New Providence in the Bahamas in search of employment. There Bonney became acquainted with a group of pirates, led by Captain John Rackam, better known as Calico Jack, with whom she later eloped and had a child, whose fate is unknown. Disguised as a man on board ship, Bonney took part in raids off Cuba and Hispaniola, joining English-born Mary Read (*c.* 1695–1721), another female member of Rackam's piratical crew. On 5 September 1720 the governor of the Bahamas issued a proclamation reporting the theft by Rackam and his associates of an armed twelve-ton sloop from New Providence, which was subsequently used for acts of piracy and robbery. The proclamation was published in the *Boston Globe* and, the following month, the vessel was intercepted off the Jamaican coast. The crew, including Bonney and Read, were captured and imprisoned in Spanish Town, Jamaica. On 16 November Rackam and his male accomplices were tried at a vice-admiralty court, where they were condemned and hanged two days later. On 28 November, at a separate trial in Spanish Town, Bonney and Read were tried for piracy. Although both women pleaded not guilty, the evidence of witnesses was incontrovertible. It was claimed that Bonney and Read were neither kept nor detained by force but that they engaged in piracy of their own free will. Eyewitnesses stated that the two women, disguised in men's clothing, were each armed with a machete and pistol and that, as one of the last defenders of the ship, Bonney was very active on board and willing to do anything.

Although pleas of pregnancy saved both women from the death penalty, Read died in prison and was buried in the Jamaican district of St Catherine on 28 April 1721. William Cormac, however, apparently secured his daughter's release from prison and Bonney returned to Charles Town, South Carolina, where she gave birth to Rackam's second child. In December 1721 she married local man Joseph Burleigh and the couple had eight children. Bonney died, aged eighty-four, in South Carolina on 25 April 1782. The exploits of Bonney and Read were dramatised by playwright Steve Gooch in *The women pirates* (1978), where they are portrayed as two women escaping from female stereotypes within a small group of anti-colonial rebel pirates.

Frances Clarke

SOURCES
Phillip Gosse, *The history of piracy* (1954); Daniel Defoe, *A general history of pyrates*, ed. M. Schonhorn (1970); Jennifer Uglow, *The Macmillan dictionary of women's biography* (1989); John C. Appleby, 'Women and piracy in Ireland: from Gráinne O'Malley to Anne Bonny', *Women in early modern Ireland*, ed. Margaret MacCurtain and Mary O'Dowd (1991), 53–68; *ODNB*

Boyd, William
1685–1772
Presbyterian minister

William Boyd was born in 1685; it is possible but not certain that his father was the Rev. Thomas Boyd (d. *c.* 1699), minister (1660–99) of Aghadowey, Co. Londonderry, who was one of the ministers ejected for non-conformity in 1661 and who survived the siege of Derry in 1689. His successor in Aghadowey was James McGregor. William Boyd graduated from the University of Edinburgh in 1702, and read divinity at Glasgow; he was licensed by the presbytery of Route in 1707 and ordained on 31 January 1710 as Presbyterian minister of Macosquin, Co. Londonderry.

In March 1718 Boyd was sent by over 300 petitioners from the Bann valley to bear their petition to Samuel Shute, colonial governor of Massachusetts and New Hampshire; discontented in Ireland, they sought Shute's backing for a planned emigration. Boyd arrived in Boston in late July 1718, and the main parties of emigrants, who had not awaited an outcome of the petition, arrived in August before any land had been allocated, though Boyd had been favourably received. Boyd remained for some months in Boston, becoming well known as a preacher, and impressing the prominent ministers Cotton and Increase Mather. An altercation in a Boston bookshop (February 1719) with a man who had accused Boyd of sexual misconduct with a maidservant in an inn did not affect Boyd's reputation; his antagonist was subsequently fined £20 7s. 0d. After giving his farewell sermon in Boston, Boyd was asked to dine with the governor, Cotton Mather, James McGregor, and the Rev. James Woodside, who had ordained him in Macosquin.

It is possible that William Boyd was related to Archibald Boyd of Maghera, Co. Londonderry, who is known to have been a minister in America with McGregor, and to Adam Boyd of Co. Antrim, who was ordained in America in 1724. William Boyd did not remain in America; he returned to Macosquin, and in 1725 accepted a call to Monreagh in Donegal, where he was installed on 25 April 1725. Problems arose when his predecessor there, without the permission of presbytery, returned to the area; he attracted many of his former hearers to his services in a disused corn kiln in St Johnstown, and despite presbytery's support for Boyd, the congregation acrimoniously split between the ministers, and Boyd's stipend was considerably reduced. He was selected as moderator of synod in 1730; his final sermon as moderator was printed, and reveals his strong support for the orthodox position against the non-subscribers, who had been grouped in their own presbytery since 1725. He held that the human conscience is subservient to the law of God as expressed in the scriptures and interpreted by the church. Boyd was one of ten ministers given the task in 1747 of drawing up a 'Serious warning' against unorthodox doctrines 'creeping into our bounds'.

He lived till 2 May 1772, in poor health for the last years of his life, and was buried in Taughboyne. He was survived by some of his children; no details of them or of his wife are known.

Linde Lunney

SOURCES

Thomas Witherow, *Historical and literary memorials of Presbyterianism in Ireland*, 2nd ser. (1880), 1–7; *DNB*; Charles Knowles Bolton, *Scotch Irish pioneers in Ulster and America* (1910, repr. 1967); McConnell, *Fasti* (1951); R. J. Dickson, *Ulster emigration to colonial America 1718–1775* (1966), 21

Burk, John Daly
1772?–1808
Author and radical

John Daly Burk was possibly the son of James Burk, a Protestant schoolmaster from Co. Cork, who may have been related to the statesman Edmund Burke (*Augusta Chronicle*, 11 November 1809). In 1790 John was appointed usher at a private school in Cork. He entered Trinity College Dublin as a sizar (5 June 1792), and claimed to have won several literary prizes there. At Trinity he read Hume, Gibbon, Price, and Priestley, and became a deist and a democrat. He wrote regularly for the anti-government *Dublin Evening Post*, including some deistical articles in 1794 which led the college authorities to expel him for blasphemy. He responded by writing *The trial of John Burk* (1794) which defended his right to religious speculation, accused the college authorities of instituting a new inquisition, and compared his persecution to that of Priestley, Galileo, and Socrates.

After his expulsion he became increasingly active in Dublin radical circles. Burk claimed to have founded the Athenian, Telegraph, and Philanthrophic societies to promote republican debate, and to have formed a new revolutionary society (possibly the reconstituted United Irishmen), with a largely artisan membership organised in cells. He also belonged to the Strugglers' Club (named after the tavern where they met). The Strugglers' had links with the Catholic secret society, the Defenders, and plotted various schemes, including the rescue of imprisoned radicals, the assassination of government agents, and an attack on Dublin Castle. Described as 'high and lofty in his carriage, haughty in his manners, and imperious and impulsive in his disposition' (cited in Durey, 114), Burk engaged in military preparations and was a prominent leader of plebeian radicals in Dublin. Wanted by the authorities, he fled to America in autumn 1796. Apparently he had been surrounded by soldiers in a Dublin bookshop but escaped by disguising himself in the clothes of a Miss Daly, whose name he adopted in gratitude.

He arrived in Boston and on 6 October 1796 started a newspaper, the *Polar Star and Boston Daily Advertiser*, characterised by its democratic and anti-British politics, which failed after five months. His radicalism also had a social dimension, and he criticised the accumulation of property and unrestricted operation of the market: just as the *Dublin Evening Post* had advocated regulating the bread trade in the mid 1790s, so the *Polar Star* violently attacked profiteering corn merchants. He moved to New York early in 1797, where he edited the radical Jeffersonian paper, the *Time Piece* (June–August 1798), and engaged in street fights against federalist opponents. Associating with exiled friends, he became involved in the American Society of United Irishmen in New York, a secret society that combined Irish and American concerns, and chaired a meeting on 4 July 1798. He idealised America as the fulfilment of his republican dream and excoriated anyone who attempted to threaten this ideal. His paper attacked the alien and sedition bills as a violation of the Bill of Rights, accused President John Adams of attempting to subvert the American revolution, and demanded that all traitors to the republic should be tarred and feathered. Denounced by federalists as an Irish rabble-rouser, he was prosecuted for seditious libel in July 1798. Through the influence of Aaron Burr, the New York republican leader whom Burk had befriended, the charges were dropped on condition he left the US. Instead, in early summer 1799 he slipped away quietly to the Jeffersonian stronghold of Amelia county, Virginia, where he took an assumed name. He was appointed principal of the newly established Jefferson College, but was accused of adultery and forced to resign. Elated by Jefferson's victory in 1801, Burk wrote to him detailing his sufferings and services to the republican cause since his arrival in America, and sought a government clerkship, but was refused. He settled in Petersburg, Virginia, and became a US citizen on 14 April 1802. He began to practise law (although he had no formal qualifications) and married a local woman, Christianna Curtis; they had one son, John Junius, who became a judge.

On his fifty-day voyage to America, John Burk had written the play 'Bunker Hill, or the death of General Warren', first performed in Boston on 17 February 1797. Dismissed by critics for its sensationalism and overblown rhetoric – one remarked that its only merit was its brevity – it none the less played to packed houses and earned $2,000 for Burk. Staged with an elaborately constructed set, novel special effects, and dramatic battle scenes, it remained a popular 4 July entertainment for over fifty years.

His other plays – none of which had the popular success of 'Bunker Hill' – include the critically acclaimed 'Female patriotism, or the death of Joan D'Arc' (1798), which transformed Joan into a modern revolutionary heroine; 'Oberon, or the siege of Mexico' (1802), and 'Bethlem Gabor' (1807), a Gothic drama set in Transylvania, based on William Godwin's novel *St Leon* (1799); Burk directed and played the lead in the latter. Other plays attributed to him are 'The death of General Montgomery' (1797), 'The innkeeper of Abbeville', and 'Which do you like best, the poor man or the lord?' He believed that theatre had a moral purpose to instil a sense of patriotism and republican virtue, and he is an important figure in the development of a distinctively American style of theatre.

In 1797 he began his epic blank verse poem on the American revolution, 'The Columbiad'; bombastic and poorly written, it remained unpublished. Turning to history, he wrote *A history of the late war in Ireland* (Philadelphia, 1799), which portrayed pre-conquest Ireland as a land of justice and learning until subjected to 600 years of English tyranny. It detailed the savage brutality of crown forces in 1798 against an innocent people goaded into rebellion, and linked together the American, French, and Irish causes in a common international struggle for liberty. His *History of Virginia* (3 vols, 1804–5; a fourth volume, completed by others, was published in 1816), portrayed Virginia as an idyll of democracy and religious tolerance. It condemned slavery, extolled the nobility of Native Americans, and claimed that both natives and slaves had been humanely treated by white Virginians. Generally well-regarded, it remained a standard and influential work until the late nineteenth century. Interested in the Ossian cult (which he sought to claim for Ireland) and in the interaction of Irish and American music styles, Burk also wrote some popular songs and a 'Historical essay on the character and antiquity of Irish songs' (*Richmond Enquirer*, 27 May 1808).

Renowned for his fiery temper, he insulted the French nation in a tavern argument with a Frenchman, Felix Conquebert, and was challenged to a duel. He was shot though the heart and died in Petersburg on 11 April 1808.

James Quinn

SOURCES
John Burk, *Trial of John Burk* … (1794); Charles Campbell (ed.), *Some materials to serve for a brief memoir of John Daly Burk* (1868); D. J. O'Donoghue, *The poets of Ireland* (1912); *Alumni Dublinensis* (1924); *DAB* (1929); Edward A. Wyatt, *John Daly Burk* (1936); J. I. Shulim, 'John Daly Burk: Irish revolutionist and American patriot', *Transactions of the American Philosophical Society*, 54/6 (Oct. 1964), 5–57; Martin Burke, 'Piecing together a shattered past', David Dickson, Dáire Keogh, and Kevin Whelan (ed.), *United Irishmen: republicanism, radicalism and rebellion*

(1993), 297–306; Nancy Curtin, *The United Irishmen* (1994), 147–8; Michael Durey, *Transatlantic radicals and the early American republic* (1997), 114–15, 138, 168, 186–7, 209, 250; David Wilson, *United Irishmen, United States: immigrant radicals in the early republic* (1998); *ANB*; Michael Glazier, *The encylopedia of the Irish in America* (1999)

Caldwell, Henry
1738–1810
Soldier and administrator

Henry Caldwell was born at Castle Caldwell, near Belleek, Co. Fermanagh, fourth son among six sons and two daughters of Sir John Caldwell, landowner, and his wife Ann, daughter of John Trench, dean of Raphoe, Co. Donegal. Henry Caldwell was educated locally and with several family tutors. In 1757 he was commissioned a lieutenant in the 69th Regiment. He took part in the capture of Louisbourg, Nova Scotia in 1758, preliminary to the capture of Quebec and the fall of French Canada in 1759. Commissioned captain in the 93rd Foot (22 January 1760), he had been attached to Gen. Wolfe's staff and was bequeathed £100 by Wolfe, who died at the battle of the Plains of Abraham. In 1764 Henry Caldwell transferred to the 34th Foot when the 93rd was disbanded, and served in the West Indies for five years as governor of Fort Augusta (1764–9), where in 1763 the magazine of the fort had been struck by lightning; its contents of 3,000 barrels of gunpowder exploded, killing *c.* 300 people. In 1774 Caldwell was named agent and lessee for the seigniory of Lauzon. In time he amassed *c.* 600,000 acres. He was lieutenant-colonel commandant of the British militia for the defence of Quebec, was sent to London with the news of the successful defence of Quebec against the Americans (1775–6), and was awarded £500. In 1776 he was made a legislative councillor for Quebec. He was appointed temporary receiver general for Lower Canada in 1784 – in effect, at this time, the chief tax collector for the country. This position was made permanent in 1794.

Although the post of receiver general was one of great importance, the salary was inadequate at $800. The position was one of high responsibility considering the great sums of money passing through the hands of the incumbent, and the salary paltry considering that the receiver general was expected to bear the expenses of circulating in the highest levels of society. The whole system of collecting taxes was in confusion at this time, and like his predecessor, Henry Caldwell tried to collect money owed for the seigneurial fees of *quint* and *lods et ventes*, but with a similar lack of success. His residences were Caldwell Manor and Belmont on the Quebec side of the St Lawrence. He married (16 May 1774) Anne, daughter of Alexander

Hamilton (d. 1768) of Newtownhamilton, Co. Armagh, MP for Killyleagh 1739–60. She was sister of Hugh Hamilton, bishop of Ossory.

Frances Brooke's *The history of Emily Montague* (1769), Canada's first novel, has as its hero Colonel Ed. Rivers, a character based on Henry Caldwell, 'a tall handsome colonel of twenty-seven'. Henry Caldwell was a founder of the Quebec Agriculture Society in 1789. In 1801 he bought all the property Gen. Murray had owned at the time of his death, and which he had leased for the past thirty years. The lands cost £10,180. In these years, as the price of wheat increased, he was able to make substantial profits since he had heavily invested in building and buying mills. He was engaged in supplying troops stationed in North America, and in 1810 sold more than 1,775,000 lb. of flour to the government for £21,822. Timber was another commodity in which Caldwell was deeply involved. His sawmills became the best known in Quebec, and his Etchemin Mills at the mouth of that river were among the largest in the country. They were so widely famed that important visitors who went to see the Chaudiere Falls were sometimes allowed to see over the Caldwell mills.

Like many of the Caldwells he was a man of tempestuous nature and a strong personality. He was frequently in conflict with the governors of the colony. He served on legislative council committees from 1786, studying the problems of the militia, highways, and communications. In 1787 he was a member of the committee on education in the province of Quebec. In 1791 Caldwell was named to the new legislative council and sat on it for the rest of his life. In July 1787 he was promoted colonel of the Quebec Battalion of the British militia and held this rank till June 1794, when he resigned.

Henry Caldwell died on 28 May 1810 at Belmont, his palatial residence near Quebec, aged 72. His funeral took place on 31 May at the Anglican cathedral of the Holy Trinity in Quebec. His wife, Anne, had died six years earlier. They had one son, John. An account of the siege of Quebec by the Americans in 1776, written by Caldwell in the form of a letter addressed to Gen. Murray, was published (Quebec, 1866) by the Literary and Historical Society of Quebec. There is a major holding of material related to Caldwell in the Canadian national archives (Library and Archives Canada), and some correspondence with his family in Ireland is in the John Rylands Library, Manchester, England.

As seigneur of Lauzon, his estate opposite Quebec, Henry Caldwell used to drive around in state, half reclining on the cushions of his carriage and with a numerous following. If on a long drive he stopped at a farmhouse, even for the light refreshment of a drink of milk, he never paid the *habitant* with anything less than a gold coin. An old man was once asked about the seigneur's status in the village. He replied with awe in his voice: *'Monsieur, il était le roi, l'empereur, du village'* (Sir, he was the king, the emperor, of the village). Thirteen years after his death, in 1823, it was discovered that Henry Caldwell had embezzled nearly £40,000 during his years in this office, including almost £8,000 from the Jesuit estates which he had managed as treasurer of a commission set up to administer them. Among the several notable soldiers produced by the family, Hume Caldwell, Frederick Caldwell, Sir James Caldwell and Charles Caldwell, aide-de-camp to Gen. Wolfe, were Henry's brothers.

John Cunningham

SOURCES
J. E. Roy, *Historie de la seigneurie de Lauzon* (6 vols, 1897); Sir J. M. LeMoine, *Maple leaves*, 7th ser. (1906), 74–90; A. G. Doughty (ed.), *The journal of Captain John Knox* (3 vols, 1914–16); Louis Le Jeune, *Dictionnaire générale de biographie …* (2 vols, 1931), i, 272–6; John B. Cunningham, *Castle Caldwell and its families* (1980), 119–27

Carleton, Sir Guy
1724–1808
1st Baron Dorchester, soldier, and colonial governor

Guy Carleton was born on 3 September 1724 in Strabane, Co. Tyrone, third son of Christopher Carleton of Newry and his wife Catherine (née Ball) from Co. Donegal. He had three brothers and three sisters. Guy Carleton was a descendent of Lancelot Carleton, a soldier from Cumberland who settled in Enniskillen in the early seventeenth century. Christopher Carleton died when Guy was about 14 years old, and his mother soon married the Rev. Thomas Skelton of Newry, a Church of Ireland rector, who is believed to have seen to Carleton's education. In 1742, at age 17, Carleton was commissioned an ensign in the earl of Rothes' regiment, the 25th Foot, and was promoted lieutenant in 1745. Carleton changed to the 1st Foot Guards on 22 July 1751 and was made captain-lieutenant and lieutenant-colonel on 18 June 1757. During the Seven Years' War (1756–63), in the summer of 1758, he served at the siege of Louisbourg in Nova Scotia, and was promoted lieutenant-colonel in the 72nd Foot.

Carleton was brought on to the staff of Gen. James Wolfe, over the objections of George II, as quartermaster-general and engineer, and was promoted colonel on 30 December 1758. He participated in the capture of Quebec (September 1759), where he was wounded. He also saw action at Port-Andro, on Belle-Île-en-Mer on the French coast (8 April 1761), and at the siege of Havana in Cuba (22 July 1762). Carleton was made lieutenant-governor of Quebec in 1766, and in the absence of the governor, he assumed administrative responsibility for the province the following year. In 1770 he returned to England on a leave of absence, during which time he was promoted major-general, was consulted by a parliamentary committee in drafting the Quebec act of 1774, and on 3 January 1775 was appointed governor of Quebec. Carleton was a success. He appointed French-Canadian Catholics to his legislative council and numerous other positions within the province, reestablished French civil law, and, under the Quebec act, allowed the Catholic church to continue its public functions. Indeed, Carleton allied himself with the Catholic clergy.

With the outbreak of hostilities in the thirteen colonies in 1775 the forces of the Continental Congress invaded Quebec, driving British troops from Montreal to Quebec city; Carleton narrowly avoided capture. Quebec was besieged for six months, but held, giving Carleton the title of 'saviour of Quebec'. In the spring British reinforcements by sea lifted the siege, although Carleton was unable to capture the retreating American army. Though criticised for this failure, Carleton was promoted lieutenant-general on 1 January 1776, made a knight of the Order of the Bath on 6 July 1776, and later was appointed governor of Charlemont fort by the king as a sinecure. Carleton's subordinate, Maj.-gen. John Burgoyne, commanded the expedition defeated at Saratoga. Carleton resigned in protest, returning to England in June 1778. On 2 March 1782 Carleton succeeded Sir Henry Clinton as commander-in-chief of British forces in North America. He had instructions to negotiate peace with the colonies, but Carleton's real task was to extract the remaining 30,000 British troops and 27,000 loyalist refugees from the northern states. He also arranged land grants for many of the loyalists settled in Nova Scotia and Quebec. Carleton sailed from New York for England in December 1783.

Carleton was appointed governor of Quebec, Nova Scotia, New Brunswick, and Newfoundland on 11 April 1786, and on 21 August he was created 1st Baron Dorchester and voted a pension of £1,000 a year. He continued to work closely with the Catholic clergy, e.g. by giving an official voice to the selection of bishops and admitting priests from France, although he had been disappointed by the lack of support from French Canadians during the American war. He was more inclined to favour the British merchants and the loyalists from America. The outbreak of war between Britain and France in 1793 complicated Dorchester's mission. Seven forts, clearly within the territory ceded to the United States, had been retained by the British in order to support both fur traders and native people. As skirmishing rose in intensity between native people and Americans, Dorchester built a new fort well into American territory in

1793 and assured the natives on 10 February 1794 that war within the year was likely. This caused alarm in the United States. The British government intended to settle with the Americans because of the war with France, and Dorchester was admonished. Indignant, Dorchester asked to be relieved of his duties on 4 September 1794. The government would have preferred that Dorchester remain at his post, but he was replaced in May 1796; on 9 July 1796 he left Canada for the last time and sailed for England.

On 12 August 1793 he had been promoted a general in the army, and back in England he moved from the 15th to the 27th Dragoons and finally to the 4th Dragoons. Dorchester had married (22 May 1772) Lady Maria Howard, daughter of Thomas, 2nd earl of Effingham. The couple had nine sons and two daughters. Dorchester acquired three residences in England, Greywell Hill, Basingstoke, Kempshot House, Basingstoke, and Stubbings House, near Maidenhead. He died at Maidenhead on 10 November 1808. Dorchester's younger brother, Thomas Carleton (born 1735, probably in Strabane), was a soldier and lieutenant-governor of New Brunswick from 1784 to 1817. Dorchester's private papers were destroyed; official correspondence can be found in the War Office and Colonial Office collections of the National Archives (Kew).

Francis M. Carroll

SOURCES
DNB; *DCB*; Victor Coffin, *The province of Quebec and the early American revolution: a study in English-American colonial history* (1896); A. G. Bradley, *Lord Dorchester* (1900; new ed. under the title *Sir Guy Carleton (Lord Dorchester)*, 1966); W. [C. H.] Wood, *The father of British Canada: a chronicle of Carleton* (1916); Reginald Coupland, *The Quebec act: a study in statesmanship* (1925); A. L. Burt, *The United States, Great Britain and British North America from the revolution to the establishment of peace after the war of 1812* (1940); id., *Guy Carleton, Lord Dorchester, 1724–1808* (1955); Pierre Benoit, *Lord Dorchester (Guy Carleton)* (1961); P. R. Reynolds, *Guy Carleton: a biography* (1980); Paul David Nelson, *General Sir Guy Carleton, Lord Dorchester: soldier-statesman of early British Canada* (2000)

Clark, Thomas
1720–92
Presbyterian minister

Thomas Clark was born in Paisley, Scotland. He was a student in 1744 in the theological hall of the Associate Presbytery of Scotland, and seems to have had some medical training; in 1745, while a student, he joined the duke of Cumberland's army to oppose Charles Edward Stuart, the Young Pretender.

In 1748 he was licensed to preach, and was sent the following year by the Associate Presbytery of Glasgow on a mission to Ulster. He proved a popular preacher, and received three calls; the synod directed that he should accept that of Ballybay (Cahans), Co. Monaghan, and he was ordained there – in a field, to accommodate the large attendance – on 23 July 1751. He was the first seceder minister to publish anything: *A brief survey of some principles maintained by the general synod of Ulster*, in which he vigorously condemned the 'New Light' tendencies of Presbyterianism, appeared before his ordination, and he continued his attacks in *New light set in a clear light* (1755). He made enemies within Presbyterianism as well as attracting many new adherents. His pamphlet *Remarks upon the manner and form of swearing by touching and kissing the Gospels* (1752) resulted from Clark's controversy on this point with the authorities; his refusal to 'kiss the calfskin' (as seceders called the practice of kissing the Bible on taking an oath) led first to a fine (1752), and in 1754 he was imprisoned for two months, accused of disloyalty by two of his own elders. He continued his ministry while in jail, but was released when the judge in the circuit court decided that the disputed method of swearing was based on use and wont, rather than on law.

After the death (18 December 1762) of his wife Elizabeth (née Nesbitt), aged 32, and because of dissatisfaction with the state of religion in his congregation, Clark decided to emigrate, and left Ireland on 10 May 1764. One son aged six died (1762) in Cahans; two sons emigrated with him, and there was also a daughter. 300 Presbyterians from Cahans and the surrounding area emigrated along with him. Clark purchased 12,000 acres for his congregation in New Perth, later known as Salem, NY, and as sole doctor as well as pastor to his people lived there till 1782, when he moved to South Carolina. He was called as first minister of the joint congregations of Cedar Springs and Long Cane in 1786; they had been settled originally by people who had emigrated from Cahans with him. Clark died on 26 December 1792 in South Carolina while working on *A pastoral and farewell letter* ..., addressed to his former congregation in Ballybay, which was published after his death.

Linde Lunney

SOURCES
James Seaton Reid, *History of the Presbyterian Church in Ireland*, iii (1867), 310–17; *DNB*; David Stewart, *The Seceders in Ireland, with annals of their congregations* (1950), 292–3; 'Personal and death notices in the *Philadelphia Public Ledger* for Monaghan, Fermanagh and Cavan 1848–1873', *Clogher Record*, xvi, no. 1 (1997), 134–5; James H. Murnane and Peadar Murnane, *At the ford of the birches: the history of Ballybay, its people and vicinity* (1999), 175–90

Clerk, Matthew
1659–1735
Presbyterian minister

Matthew Clark was born near Kilrea, Co. Londonderry. He attended Glasgow University around 1679, and survived the siege of Derry (1689), where he held the rank of lieutenant and suffered a head wound; he afterwards wore a black patch over the site of the injury. After the siege he studied for the ministry, and was ordained (1697) in the congregation at Kilrea (known at that date as Boveedy). He strongly supported orthodoxy during the controversy over subscription: in 1721 he was the sole opponent of the 'Charitable declaration', in which the synod had enjoined forbearance of the non-subscribing ministers; he desired that his disapproval should be entered in the minutes. The following year, two other ministers joined his protest against compromise with the non-subscribers, and in June 1722 he published the vigorous pamphlet *Letter from the country* against the position adopted by the supporters of the Belfast Society. He followed up his attack in another pamphlet (1723), which was his reply to a letter from six members of the Belfast Society; he was the first author in the controversy on either side to use his own name on his publications.

On 29 April 1729 Clerk resigned from Kilrea; he emigrated to America and made his way to Londonderry, New Hampshire, where his old friend James McGregor had been minister. McGregor had died less than two months previously, and Clerk, without being formally installed, became minister in his place. McGregor's widow became his third wife and he undertook the education of McGregor's son David, who became a prominent minister in New England. In his last illness Clerk requested that his body should be borne to burial by old comrades from the siege of Derry, who had accompanied McGregor from Aghadowey to New Hampshire. He died on 25 January 1735. Anecdotes and a portrait are preserved in Parker's *History of Londonderry, New Hampshire*, which records that Clerk (unusually, in that period) refused to eat food of animal origin, and that he was always strongly moved by memories of his military service. While sitting as clerk of the Route presbytery, he was inattentive to those around him when a military band struck up outside; his reply to their urging was: 'Nae business while I hear the toot o' the drum'. His military instincts were also obvious when he averred that the apostle Peter had been remiss in the garden of Gethsemane: 'swaggerin aboot wi a sword at his side an a puir han he mad o it when he cam to the trial for he only cut off a chiel's lug and he ought to ha split doon his heid' (Witherow, 245–6).

Linde Lunney

SOURCES
Thomas Witherow, *Historical and literary memorials of Presbyterianism in Ireland*, 1st ser. (1880), 241–8; J. W. Kernohan, *Two Ulster parishes: Kilrea and Tamlaght O'Crilly* (1912), 55; McConnell, *Fasti*

Clinton, Charles
1690–1773
Colonist in America

Charles Clinton was born in Co. Longford on an estate granted to his family for service in the Williamite army. His father was James Clinton, a descendant of the earl of Lincoln, and his mother was Elizabeth Clinton, née Smith. One chronicler has suggested that his paternal grandfather, an adherent of King Charles I, fled to Ireland after the defeat of the royalists, and that his maternal grandfather was a captain in the army of Oliver Cromwell.

Charles Clinton was an elder of the Presbyterian congregation at Corboy, Co. Longford, and helped to organise a group exodus to North America. His title 'Colonel' (he was either in the militia or at some time in the regular army) would suggest that he had some social standing in the county. His diary gives an insight into the appalling conditions that travellers faced on their outward voyage to the New World. They set sail from Dublin on 9 May 1729 and reached America on 4 October (twenty-three weeks later). It would seem that measles or some similar acute viral infection broke out, and Clinton recorded the names of eighty-three passengers who died on the voyage, including two of his own children. Given that ships of this date carried an average of 150 passengers one can surmise that about half of Clinton's Corboy pilgrims died en route. Another, less convincing account, suggests that the captain of the ship tried to starve the passengers in order to obtain their goods.

In spring 1731 Clinton and his party reached Ulster County, sixty miles (96 km) north of New York, and settled there. He purchased a tract of land and became a farmer and land surveyor. Clinton became a useful and respected member of the colony and served as a JP and as county judge. He also drew on his earlier military experience and became lieutenant-colonel in the Ulster County militia; he served under Col. Bradstreet at the siege and capture of Fort Frontenac from the French in 1758.

His children had important military and political careers in America. His eldest son, Alexander (b. *c.* 1730), graduated at the University of Princeton and became a physician; his second son, Charles, was an army surgeon and served in the Havana campaign in 1762; the third son, James (b. 1736), pursued a military career and reached the rank of colonel in 1775 and brigadier-general in 1776. Clinton's fourth son, George (b. 1739), was also in the army and served alongside his father and brother James at the capture of Fort Frontenac. He was elected to the New York assembly (1768) and the New York Provincial Congress (1777). From 1804 to 1812 he served as vice-president of the United States. Charles Clinton and his sons demonstrated their loyalty to the crown during the wars against France in the 1750s and 1760s, but the Clintons became fierce defenders of the 'liberties of their country' and opposed Britain during the imperial war of 1775–83.

Charles Clinton married Elizabeth Denniston in Ireland; they had five sons and two daughters. He died in Orange County, New York, on 19 November 1773. Some Clinton family papers are held at the New York State Library.

Daniel Beaumont

SOURCES
Clinton family papers, New York State Library, MS NYOR 599-880-0002; *Appletons*, i, 658–9; *DNB*; T. J. Barron, 'The Presbyterian exodus from Co. Longford in 1729', *Breifne*, v (1977–8), 253–7; Liam Kennedy et al., 'The long retreat: protestants, economy and society, 1660–1926', Raymond Gillespie and Gerard Moran (ed.), *Longford: essays in county history* (1991)

Craghead family
Presbyterian ministers

Robert Craghead, or Craighead, (1633–1711) was born in Scotland, probably in the east of the country, and graduated MA (1653) from St Andrews University. He was licensed as a commonwealth minister in the parish church of Donaghmore, Co. Donegal, and received the tithes of the parish in December 1658; in 1661 he was deposed for nonconformity, but continued to minister there for many years as a minister of the Laggan presbytery. In 1689 he moved to Derry city, where he was to become minister of First Derry; however, on the second day of the siege of the city (April 1689) he and some of his family fled to Scotland. They were robbed en route of all their possessions by Jacobite soldiers. He was allocated a church in Glasgow, but he returned to Derry when the siege ended, and was installed in First Derry on 1 July 1690, the same day as the battle between the two kings, James II and William III, at the River Boyne. In reply to several attacks on Presbyterians by William King, bishop of Derry, Craghead published pamphlets in the 1690s in which he forcefully upheld Presbyterian forms of worship. The bishop had, according to Craghead, depicted Presbyterians 'as black as heathens ... degenerate and barbarous', and in defiance of the bishop's views on civic government, the minister expressly defended the mayor and burgesses of the city, mostly dissenters, who were generally unwilling to take communion in the established church as demanded by the act of uniformity. Like most inter-sect arguments of the period, the controversy, though couched in theological terms, had political implications. Craghead was asked by synod to prepare materials on the history of the church; nothing is known of any outcome. His *Advice to communicants* (1698) was so well regarded that it was reprinted in Glasgow (1714, 1758) and in Philadelphia (1792, 1838). Craghead spent a short time in Glasgow (1698–9) as minister of Blackfriars church, but returned to Derry, and died there on 27 August 1711.

His wife was Agnes, daughter of the Rev. John Hart of Taughboyne, another minister who was ejected for nonconformity, and who was one of four ministers who had suffered an imprisonment of six years because he had refused to obey a summons to attend the bishop's court. Robert and Agnes Craghead are believed to have had eight children: four daughters, including Katherine, who married the Rev. William Homes and emigrated with him to New England, and four sons.

One son was **Robert Craighead** junior (1684–1738), born probably in Donaghmore, who received an excellent education, first in philosophy and then in divinity, at the universities of Glasgow, Edinburgh, and Leiden; he graduated MA from Leiden in 1702. He was licensed by Derry presbytery, and ordained as minister of Capel Street congregation (later known as Abbey) in Dublin on 11 October 1709. He was elected moderator of general synod in 1719, and was thus the outgoing moderator in 1720 – the year in which the subscription controversy, which was to become one of the most important and divisive issues in the history of Presbyterianism, was first brought before the synod in Ireland. Though his own beliefs were orthodox trinitarian, Craighead' s sermon on the occasion, afterwards printed as *A plea for peace* ... , recommended toleration of those who reserved the right not to subscribe to human formulations of doctrine, in the interests of promoting church harmony, and the synod subsequently passed the 'Pacific act' in 1720. Neither this act, nor many further discussions of the matter over many years, succeeded in producing the harmony sought by Craighead. In 1728 Craighead, with two other Dublin ministers, Francis Iredell and Richard Choppin, prepared an address to the king, in which they noted that great numbers of Presbyterians (including Craighead's own brother and his family) had gone to find in America 'that liberty and ease ... denied in their native country'. They sought the assistance of the London government in mitigating the conditions under which dissenters lived, and particularly cited the obnoxious sacramental test. In the spring of 1729 Iredell and Craighead were asked by the lords justices of Ireland to prepare a report on the matter; they consulted all the northern presbyteries, and presented a fuller analysis of the causes of emigration, including economic as well as religio-political motivation. Craighead visited London in 1729 and 1731 in connection with the presentation of the memorial to government, and with support from Archbishop Hugh Boulter successfully lobbied for payment of arrears of *regium donum*, the king's bounty first paid to Presbyterian ministers in 1672. The civil and political liberties sought by his co-religionists were, however, still denied by the Dublin government. Craighead died in Dublin on 30 July 1738 after a lingering illness; there is no record of any marriage or family, but his congregation and friends mourned his loss.

Another son of Robert and Agnes Craghead was **Thomas Craghead** (d. 1739), born in Donaghmore, possibly around 1670, though one source says about 1664. He is said to have married (1690) Margaret Wallace in Scotland, and he graduated MA from Edinburgh (1691), was licensed by Laggan presbytery, and was ordained in Ballintra and Castlederg (6 July 1698). He resigned Ballintra in 1710, and in 1714, with testimonials from Ulster, emigrated with his family and with his sister Katherine Homes, her husband, the Rev. William Homes, and family to New England. The westwards migration of Ulster Presbyterians in America, from the New England seaboard to the frontier in Pennsylvania, is reflected in the shifting ministry of Thomas Craghead. In 1715 he was installed as minister of Freetown, Massachusetts. On 22 September 1724 he was installed in White Clay Creek, Delaware. He was almost certainly one of the six ministers who in 1729 formed a committee of synod to draft a report on the need to impose upon ministerial candidates a subscription to the Westminster confession; the 'adopting act' of 1729, which was passed as a result, is regarded as one of the most important events in the early history of the American Presbyterian church. He resigned after nine years in Delaware; was installed in Pequea, in the presbytery of Donegal, Pennsylvania (31 October 1733); resigned in 1736; and was installed in Hopewell congregation, Pennsylvania (October 1738). In 1736 the session of Pequea complained that the minister had barred his wife Margaret from receiving communion because of 'a dreadful delusion of Satan, if not a delirium in his head'; the session's complaint was on account of the minister's failure to consult them before debarring her, as required in church law and usage. The presbytery ordered her to be admitted to communion in the congregation again, and Craghead reluctantly did so. He died on 26 April 1739, while preaching in the pulpit of Hopewell church. Thomas and Margaret Craghead are said to have had four sons and a daughter Jane, who married the Rev. Adam Boyd (1692–1768), one of the first Presbyterian ministers in Pennsylvania, who was from Co. Antrim, and may have been a brother of the Rev. William Boyd (d. 1772).

One of Thomas and Margaret's sons, **Alexander Craighead** (*c.* 1707–66), born in Ireland, was seven or eight years old when he went to America with his family and his aunt's family, arriving in Boston in October 1715. They lived in Massachusetts, Delaware, and then in Pennsylvania, where he most likely received some of his education from the Rev. William Tennent (1673–1745). It is certain that he was strongly influenced by the 'New Side' tendency in American Presbyterianism of the time, which was associated with many of those trained by William Tennent, including Gilbert Tennent, Samuel Blair, and Samuel Finley. These men advocated a revival of religion on evangelical principles, and particularly stressed the need for a ministry by those who had experienced conversion, rather than those who had, as they claimed, merely theoretical knowledge of divine grace. Craighead passed without distinction the necessary presbytery examinations before being licensed by the presbytery of Donegal on 8 October 1734. He was installed in Middle Octorara (Octoraro) in Lancaster County, Pennsylvania (18 November 1735); he was the first Presbyterian minister west of the Susquehanna river. In the 1740s he was deeply involved in the Great Awakening in the American churches, a revival of religion which grew in part from the exhortatory evangelism of such itinerants as the Englishman George Whitefield. Craighead accompanied Whitefield on some of his preaching tours in Chester County, Pennsylvania, in November 1739; it is said that the woods rang with the praise hymns they sang as they rode. The schism between the 'Old Side' and the 'New Side' widened rapidly at this time; the 'Old Side', often though not always older ministers, did not particularly relish this revival, and resented the intrusion into their congregations of the enthusiasm and charismatic preaching of ministers from other congregations and even other presbyteries, who frequently addressed unprecedentedly large congregations out of doors. In 1740 Craighead intruded into the congregations of Francis Alison and John Thomson, and charges were brought against him and another minister at the meeting of Donegal presbytery in Middle Octorara in September 1740. Angry crowds 'railing at the members in the most scurrilous and opprobrious terms' prevented his trial by presbytery from taking place until the meeting adjourned to a private house; the two ministers admitted intruding, but refused to desist; the presbytery minutes state that 'we have not known a parallel instance [of defiance] since we have been capable to mark any thing in the world.' Craighead was suspended, but refused to accept the verdict because he had been tried by the same body that had accused him. He continued to preach and to minister; in 1743 he administered the Scottish covenant to his congregation in Octorara. He then urged Synod to call for a renewal of the covenant as an antidote to contemporary falling away of religion; in 1743 the synod accused him of censoriousness and rejected his efforts to reintroduce covenanting zeal. He described the events in Octorara in a publication, *Renewal of the covenants national and solemn league …* (1748). Benjamin Franklin was the printer, and also printed Craighead's *The reasons for … receding from the present judiciaries of the church* (1743). Craighead is thus closely linked with the concept of a covenanted polity and with the reluctance to pay allegiance to non-covenanted leaders which had characterised the Scottish covenanters, and which some scholars trace in the intellectual climate that produced the American Declaration of Independence (1776).

The New Side emphasised the importance of outreach to the frontier communities, and Alexander Craighead moved with hundreds of other Scotch-Irish settlers down the Shenandoah valley. Perhaps by 1749, and certainly by March 1753, he was living on a large tract of land by the Cowpasture river in Virginia, and was minister of Windy Cove, where the congregation was under constant threat of Indian attack, and went armed to church. He moved in January 1758 to Mecklenburg County, North Carolina, and was the first pastor from November 1758 of Sugar Creek and Rocky River churches, in an area settled largely by the Scotch-Irish, which developed later into the city of Charlotte. Partisan authors claim to detect Craighead's influence on the radical 'Mecklenburg resolves' of May 1775; but since Craighead himself had died on 12 March 1766, it is only the known presence at the drafting convention of numerous Presbyterians who had been Craighead's hearers that can be adduced as evidence for any effects of his covenanting theology on the advanced political thought in the region. A putative document of the same time, known as the 'Mecklenburg declaration of independence', which is said to have pre-dated and perhaps influenced the much more famous Jeffersonian document, may also have incorporated Craighead's views, but since no contemporary copy is extant, this is even less capable of proof.

The minister seems to have married first (*c.* 1734) Agnes Brown, in Pennsylvania; she may have died after the birth of her second daughter. He married secondly a Miss Scott; they had four or five daughters and two sons. Shortly before his death (perhaps in 1764 or 1765), he married Jean Martin, who may have been daughter of a minister. They seem not to have had any children.

American descendants of Robert and Agnes Craghead are numerous, and include many people prominent in later American Presbyterianism. Another grandson of Thomas and Margaret Craighead was the Rev. John Craighead (1742–99), a minister in Pennsylvania who raised a company of soldiers within his congregation to fight in the American War of Independence; as chaplain, he is said to have 'preached and fought alternately' (Craighead, 336). One of Alexander's sons was founding principal of Davidson Academy, Tennessee, later to become Nashville

University, and founding minister of the first Presbyterian church in Nashville; the other son was one of the first settlers in the city of Knoxville, Tennessee. Robert's grandson, George Craighead, was said to have been an intimate friend of George Washington.

Linde Lunney

SOURCES

Robert Craghead, *The true terms of Christian and ministerial communion ...*, *containing a short account of the author by Mr Abernethy* (1739); James Seaton Reid, *History of the Presbyterian Church in Ireland*, ii (1867), 425–33; James Geddes Craighead, *The Craighead family: a genealogical memoir of the descendants of Rev. Thomas and Margaret Craighead 1658–1876* (1876); J. G. Craighead, *Scotch and Irish seeds in American soil* (1878), 298; C. Huston Irwin, *History of Presbyterianism in Dublin and the south and west of Ireland* (1890), 55, 62–4, 266; Alexander G. Lecky, *The Laggan and its Presbyterianism* (1905), 21; Archibald Henderson, 'The Mecklenburg declaration of independence', *Journal of American History* (1912); Guy S. Klett, *Presbyterians in colonial Pennsylvania* (1937); McConnell, *Fasti* (1951); Catalog of the Library of Congress; David W. Hall, 'On the hermeneutics of subscription', *Premise*, ii, no. 1 (1995), 8–13; Tommy Lee, 'Presbyterians and revivalism ...' (1997) (at www.homes.org/ theologia/papers/tlee_presbyterians_and_revivalism.html); Anon., 'The Scottish covenanting struggle, Alexander Craighead and the Mecklenburg declaration' (at http://members.aol.com/Lettermen2/Craig.html); History of Rocky River Presbyterian church (at www.rockyriver.org/history/pastor.html); Peter J. Wallace, 'Old Light on the New Side: John Thomson and Gilbert Tennent on the Great Awakening' (at www.nd.edu/pwallace/thomson.txt); family information from Phillips Verner Bradford, family historian, at www.concentric.net; family information at www.riggenbach.org/html (all internet sources accessed Oct. 2000); family information from Ben Grimes, family historian, and from Janine Bentley

Crawford, John
1746–1813
Doctor, medical publisher, and public benefactor

John Crawford was born on 3 May 1746 at Ballytromery near Crumlin, Co. Antrim, second son among six children of Thomas Crawford (d. 1782), Presbyterian minister and farmer, and Anne Crawford (née Mackay). His elder brother was William Crawford (d. 1800), a prominent Presbyterian minister; Adair Crawford, a doctor and chemist, and Alexander Crawford (d. 1823), a doctor and United Irishman, were younger brothers, and they had two sisters. Thomas Crawford senior was himself son and grandson of Presbyterian divines noted in their day; he was minister in Crumlin from 1724 until his death, and farmed the congregational farm. Anne Crawford was the aunt of the novelist Elizabeth Hamilton (d. 1816) and of Charles Hamilton, an orientalist (d. 1792).

John Crawford was educated locally, perhaps by his father; he is said to have attended lectures at Trinity College Dublin from about the age of seventeen, but an assertion that he graduated there is unconfirmed. He was probably apprenticed to a Dublin doctor, and between 1772 and 1774 he was surgeon on board the East India Company ship *Marquis of Rockingham* on voyages to Bombay and Bengal; he seems also to have visited China and St Helena. In 1772 he published an account of a liver disease fatal in hot climates, which may have been beriberi. He possibly visited Ireland around 1778; around that time he married Mary, daughter of John O'Donnell and Barbara O'Donnell (née Anderson) of Trough, on the border of Co. Clare and Co. Limerick. It is possible that he met her through knowing her brothers in the East India Company: John O'Donnell (died after 1805?) had an adventurous career in the east before becoming a very prominent merchant in Baltimore, Maryland, and Henry Anderson O'Donnell (b. 1758) married a Persian princess.

Crawford and his wife went to Barbados, on his appointment as surgeon to the hospital there. When a hurricane in 1780 devastated the island, Crawford could have made a great deal of money from his surviving supplies of food and medicine, but instead gave them away to those in need. His health broke down due to overwork and exposure, and in 1782 he and his wife and two small children travelled to England on furlough, but his wife died on the voyage. Crawford was forced to leave his children behind in England when he returned to Barbados in 1786. In 1790 he became surgeon-major in Demerara, then a Dutch colony, and in 1794, on a visit to Europe, he took his MD in the Dutch university of Leiden; the University of St Andrews had granted him the degree of MD in 1791.

John O'Donnell, Crawford's brother-in-law, suggested that he and his children should settle in Baltimore, Maryland, and in 1796 he moved there. He found himself among 'more of the branches of the families amidst of which I was born than I have ever seen since I left my native country' (quoted in Wilson (1942)), and was made most welcome. He was friendly with the famous doctor Benjamin Rush, and established a good practice. He enthusiastically studied the natural history of his new environment, as he had done in the tropics; he had a wide knowledge of botany and entomology. Even before 1794, when he discussed his ideas with the medical faculty in Leiden, he had come to the conclusion that insects at various stages of their life-cycles could be vectors of diseases in humans. This had been suggested in outline by earlier authors, but a theory of the role of 'animalculae' in the spread of disease had never found any backing, as it was contrary to the then generally accepted doctrine that fevers and agues resulted from exposure to miasma (the very name of malaria still expresses this long-held idea) or from simple contagion. Crawford was first to suggest that insects were involved in the spread of yellow fever. Other medical men poured scorn on his novel ideas, and his practice and reputation suffered.

In 1804 Crawford started publishing a weekly magazine, the *Companion and Weekly Miscellany*, using the pseudonym of Edward Easy, and in 1806 transferred the editorship to his daughter Eliza, who thus became the second woman editor in the United States. In this weekly, retitled *The Observer and Repertory ...*, he published during 1806–7 his 'Theory and application to the treatment of disease'. Some notice was taken of his ideas, but he found no adherents. Even in 1811, when he planned a course of lectures on the cause and treatment of diseases, he was not hopeful of convincing his opponents. He wrote to Benjamin Rush that 'my situation can not be made worse by it ... My contemporaries may not thank me for the attempt; I know they will not: my great aim is to do good, and I leave the issue to him from whom I have received what I have' (quoted in Wilson), and in the published version of the only lecture that is known to have been delivered he pledged that as long as 'life and health remain, I shall devote myself strictly to the performance of my duty'. A number of palliative and curative measures for use in epidemic diseases, involving *inter alia* rigorous hygiene of the sickroom, were suggested by Crawford on the basis of his theory; some are now established as routine medical practice, though his opposition to any idea of contagion as a means of infection vitiates a few of his recommendations.

As well as his importance as a pioneer of a theory of insect-borne disease, Crawford is recognised as one of the two doctors who first introduced vaccination against smallpox into America. In the summer of 1800, at the same time as Benjamin Waterhouse was also experimenting with cowpox, Crawford received vaccine from London, and apparently successfully vaccinated at least one person. He published nothing on his vaccination work, but rejoiced in 1807 that smallpox had been rendered nearly harmless by the new technique. Crawford was involved with other projects to benefit his fellow citizens in Baltimore: he was one of the founders of Baltimore Library (1798) and of a Society for the Promotion of Useful Knowledge in the city (1800). He helped to establish a dispensary in Baltimore (1801) and a state penitentiary, and suggested improvements in training military and naval medical men. He was consulting physician to the Baltimore hospital, an examiner in the Baltimore medical faculty, and briefly (1812) held a lectureship in natural history in Baltimore Medical College. He was prominent in the city's Hibernian Society, and was grand master of the Masonic order in Maryland in every year but one from 1801 until his death, which took place on 9 May 1813. He was buried with

Masonic honours in Westminster Presbyterian graveyard in Baltimore; James McHenry (1753–1816), also a doctor, a Mason, and from Co. Antrim, is buried in the same place. Crawford's valuable and important library was bought by the University of Maryland at auction in 1813; the first major book purchase of that institution, it forms the nucleus of what is now known as the Health Sciences and Human Services Library.

Crawford's daughter Eliza survived him; she had led an adventurous life, having travelled to France as companion to Elizabeth Patterson (1785–1879), first wife of Jérôme Bonaparte (1784–1860). Eliza Crawford married first Henry Anderson, probably a relative, then left him and married secondly Maximilian Godefroy, a noted architect. Crawford lived with them from their marriage (1799) until his death. He and his daughter are described by Elizabeth McCalmont (née Barklie) of Larne, Co. Antrim, in memoirs published by Francis J. Bigger. Crawford's son seems to have trained in medicine in London, but may have died of consumption before his father.

Linde Lunney

SOURCES
F. J. Bigger, *The Magees of Belfast and Dublin, printers* ... (1916), 33; John Rathbone Oliver, 'An unpublished autograph letter from Dr John Crawford (1746–1813) to General William Henry Winder (1775–1824)', *Bulletin of the Institute of the History of Medicine*, iv (1930), 145–51; *DAB*; Julia E. Wilson, 'An early Baltimore physician and his medical library', *Annals of Medical History*, 3rd ser., iv (1942), 63–80; Burke, *Landed gentry of Ireland* (1958), 186, 533; Davis Coakley, *Irish masters of medicine* (1992), 47–54; *ANB*; 'John Crawford 1746–1813' (website of Health Sciences and Human Services Library, University of Maryland, www.hshsl.umaryland.edu/resources/historical/crawford/biography.html (accessed Feb. 2004))

Dobbs, Arthur
1689–1765
Politician and colonial governor

Arthur Dobbs was born on 2 April 1689 in Girvan, Ayrshire, Scotland, second son of Richard Dobbs of Castle Dobbs, Carrickfergus, Co. Antrim, and Mary Dobbs (née Stewart) of Ballintoy, Co. Antrim. His father was an army captain serving in the Co. Antrim Williamite association in 1689 and had sent his pregnant wife to Scotland for safety. Arthur's education may either have taken place at home with tutors (perhaps including Jonathan Swift in 1695–6) or in England, and in 1711 he purchased a cornetcy in Echlin's Dragoons and went to Scotland to serve. He succeeded his father in the Castle Dobbs estate in March 1711 and retired from the army a year later on half pay. On 12 May 1719 he married Anne Osburn Norbury, a widow, who brought an estate in Co. Kildare with her; they had six children.

Dobbs had small estates which he strove to improve, but he also had political ambitions. In 1720 he was elected mayor of Carrickfergus and appointed sheriff of Co. Antrim, all under the patronage of Lord Conway. In 1727 he was elected MP for Carrickfergus, after a contest that cost him at least £1,000, and the following year was again elected mayor and appointed deputy governor of the town. Dobbs needed greater patronage in order to advance, and sought this through his ideas for the improvement of Ireland in a British and imperial context. In 1729 he published the first part of *An essay on the trade and improvement of Ireland*, a two-part statistical work on trade. This book is, in many ways, the key to understanding Dobbs's career. It was written between 1728 and 1731 at a time when the Irish economy was in a deep crisis and there was much agonising from such writers as Jonathan Swift, Thomas Prior and others. Dobbs was much less of a propagandist than most of the pamphleteers, concentrating less on Ireland's ills than on remedies for them.

This work and, more importantly, his loyalty to the government brought him to the attention of Archbishop Hugh Boulter, who in March 1730 introduced Dobbs to the prime minister, Sir Robert Walpole. Dobbs went to London armed with a memorandum arguing for aggressive imperial administration and expansion to curb French plans in North America and, though this was hardly to Walpole's tastes, he did give Dobbs an introduction to London merchant circles and secured for him the agency to the Conway estates in Antrim. This patronage also helped, in 1733, to gain him the post of surveyor general of Ireland, worth £300 a year. Walpole's interest may also have spurred on Dobbs to pursue the twin objects of improvement of Ireland through union, and British advances in North America. He was a founder member of the Dublin Society in 1731, published the second part of the *Essay on trade* in 1732 and, one year later, circulated a manuscript arguing for union. The second object quickly involved him in plans to launch an expedition to find a north-west passage, and into controversy with the Hudson's Bay Company. In 1741 the first expedition took place; it ended in acrimony and failure (at least in finding the passage, if not in mapping Hudson's Bay). Dobbs spent much of the 1740s pamphleteering against both the captain of the first expedition and the Hudson's Bay Company, inveighing against both monopolies and complacency about the French and the providential path of imperial expansion. A second expedition (1746–7) was undertaken by his raising almost £10,000 in subscriptions, but again there was no triumph.

Though the north-west passage remained elusive, Dobbs did not lose interest in the empire. He turned his attention southwards to North

Carolina as his London friends involved him in the purchase of 400,000 acres in that colony in 1745. After the lands were properly surveyed he organised two emigrant ships (April 1751, May 1753) to take at least 500 Irish Protestant emigrants to North Carolina. The Ohio valley was another area of land speculation for Dobbs, as he and his London contacts bought 200,000 acres there and formed the Ohio Company in 1750 to survey and colonise the area. The death of his wife, Anne, in April 1747 certainly made him lose some interest in imperial endeavours but it also loosened his ties to Ireland. So, it was little surprise that Dobbs should lobby to replace the deceased Gabriel Johnston as governor of North Carolina from 1752. After six months in London the Pelham government granted Dobbs the post in January 1753, again surely helped by his circulating of manuscripts about union of Ireland with Britain and his published works on North America and the need for expansion to combat French ambitions.

At age 65 Dobbs left Ireland for North America in June 1754 with some family members and muskets and cannon for the defence of North Carolina. His rule of the colony combined the aims of regulating the rapid expansion of North Carolina and bringing it into the British mainstream with Anglican churches and schools. The main problem was the French and Indian threat in 1754, which was soon to overrun the Ohio valley and lead to the Seven Years' War, starting (in Europe) in 1756. Dobbs moved from New Bern to Russellborough (near Brunswick) and built a second Castle Dobbs there, in 1758. His governorship was successful, in that North Carolina easily defended itself during the war with the French, but by 1760 he had run into problems with the colonists. Part of the reason for this was Dobbs's desire to run an administration above the factional divides between the northern and southern elites in the colony. The other major difficulty was that Dobbs, being a proprietor himself, was hardly free from prejudice as he favoured his old London colleagues over other landowners in the north of the colony. Then, in 1760, when the northerners petitioned for his removal, he openly embraced the southern planters, packing the colonial council with supporters and marrying the fifteen-year-old southern heiress Justina Davis, from Brunswick. His colonial career ended in November 1762 with a stroke, though it was only in the following spring he applied for leave to retire. Dobbs's health did improve, as he was nursed by his new wife, but another stroke on 28 March 1765 proved fatal. He was buried in St Philip's church, Brunswick, though no Anglican minister could be found to perform the service.

Dobbs's surviving manuscripts include letters, essays, and memorandums (Public Record Office of Northern Ireland, D/162); an essay on union, *c.* 1733 (National Library of Ireland); and a manuscript on the north-west passage, *c.* 1741 (Glasgow University Library).

Eoin Magennis

41

SOURCES
D. Clarke, *Arthur Dobbs, Esquire* (1957); D. H. Rankin and E. C. Nelson (ed.), *Curious in everything: the career of Arthur Dobbs of Carrickfergus* (1990); *ANB*, vi (1999)

Dongan, Thomas
1634–1715
2nd earl of Limerick, soldier and first governor of New York

Thomas Dongan (D'Unguent) was third son of Sir John Dongan, baronet, of Castletown Kildrought (Celbridge), Co. Kildare, and his wife Mary, daughter of Sir William Talbot, baronet, of Carton, and niece of Peter Talbot, archbishop of Dublin, and Richard Talbot, earl of Tyrconnell. After the execution of King Charles I his father fled to France; there the young Thomas obtained a commission as colonel in the French army, where his name was usually spelt D'Unguent. He participated in Turenne's campaigns against Spain, where he first made the acquaintance of James, duke of York (later King James II). Dongan remained in the French service after the restoration and was colonel of an Irish regiment in 1674, a commission worth £5,000 a year. When King Charles II in 1677 commanded all his subjects to leave the French service, Dongan's acquiescence displeased Louis XIV, who swiftly banished him from France, thereby forcing him to forgo an outstanding debt of 65,000 livres which the king owed him for recruits and arrears of pay. Charles II rewarded him with a pension of £500 a year (which he never got) and the commission of major-general in the army of Flanders. Unable to take up his posting due to the peace of Nijmegen, he became lieutenant-governor of Tangier under the 2nd earl of Inchiquin.

In 1682 he received a vice-admiral's commission and became the first governor of the duke of York's province of New York, probably thanks to his knowledge of Dutch and French and to the rising influence of Richard Talbot at court. Dongan reached New York on 25 August and immediately set about organising the provincial government. He called the freeholders of the province to an assembly and granted it a charter of liberties, which attempted to make them coequal and independent of the English parliament and included a clause guaranteeing liberty of conscience. Dongan also spearheaded the transformation of New York from the struggling Dutch settlement of 207 houses (New Amsterdam) into a thriving commercial town. In 1686 he presented it with a charter ('Dongan's charter') which has remained the basis of the municipal laws, rights, privileges, public property, and franchise in New York City. This document, housed in the New York Public Library, is the city's most precious documentary possession. He also managed to make peace (1684) between the crown and the five nations of the Iroquois confederacy, bringing them under Charles II's suzerainty, while defending their interests against French aggression. In 1688 he settled a number of Irish on Long Island and along the Hudson river in Dutchess and Columbia counties.

Ignominiously dismissed from his post in 1688, possibly as a result of increasing French influence at court and of James's belief that New York would not need a governor when joined to the dominions of New England, he retired to his estate of Castleton, in Staten Island. He refused offers of employment in England and Ireland from James and Tyrconnell, unlike his eldest brother, William Dongan, earl of Limerick, who was attainted for his support for James II, with his estates passing to the Williamite commander Godard van Reede van Ginkel. Thomas Dongan then returned to America. On the death of his brother William in 1698, having succeeded him as 2nd earl of Limerick, Thomas returned to England to petition for the forfeited estate.

Thomas spent his declining years attempting to retain his ancestral lands. In 1700 the English parliament passed an act of resumption of all grants of the Irish forfeitures and vested them in trustees. Dongan petitioned the English parliament for relief and it finally passed a bill giving him liberty to claim his estate. He was strongly opposed by Henry Westenra and others who had paid Ginkel £8,000 for his grant of the estate. However, the earl could not collect his sizeable arrears of rent or regain rectory and tithe lands, and he had to reimburse two-thirds of the money to those who had purchased his estate from Ginkel. The resulting financial burdens forced him to sell the estate at Castletown in 1709 to William 'Speaker' Conolly (1662–1729), leaving nothing but the empty title.

Dongan was one of the prominent Irish Catholic aristocrats who met Father Ambrose O'Connor, Jacobite agent of the queen dowager Mary of Modena, who had been sent in 1708 on a fact-finding mission on behalf of the young Stuart claimant (the Old Pretender). Although more than willing to stress his loyalty to the cause, Limerick urged O'Callaghan not to draw Protestant suspicion on to himself or his fellow aristocrats.

The earl of Limerick died on 14 December 1715 and was buried in St Pancras graveyard, London. Survived by his wife Mary (d. 18 November 1720; buried in St James's, Westminster), he bequeathed his New York property in Broadway, New York, to his nephews Thomas, John, and Walter Dongan, sons of his brother Colonel Michael Dongan. The earldom became extinct after his death. His portrait is in the possession of the New-York Historical Society.

Éamonn Ó Ciardha

SOURCES
'Mémoir au sujet de l'entreprise sur l'Irlande' (Bibliothèque National, fonds français., vol. 7487, f. 171; National Library of Ireland, microfilm positive 102); 'Case of Thomas, earl of Limerick', *Journal of the Royal Society of Antiquaries of Ireland*, iv (1860–61), 9–11; J. C. O'Callaghan, *Irish brigades in the service of France* (1870), 332; J. S. O'Grady, 'Col. T. Dongan of Castletown-Kildrought, soldier and statesman', *Journal of Kildare Archaeological Society*, iv (1903–05), 366–9; M. Van Rensselaer, *History of New York in the seventeenth century* (2 vols, 1909), ii, 209–331; R. Hayes, *Biographical dictionary of Irishmen in France* (1949); G.E.C., *Complete Peerage*, vii, 661; P. W. Browne, 'Thomas Browne, soldier and statesman', *Studies: an Irish Quarterly Review*, xxiii (1934), 489–501; J. G. Simms, *The Williamite confiscation in Ireland 1690–1703* (1956), 139, 141, 146; M. de la Poer Beresford, 'Ireland in the French strategy 1691–1789' (M.Litt. thesis, Dublin, 1975), 20–23; A. M. Shea and M. R. Case, *The Irish experience in New York city: a select bibliography* (1995); Éamonn Ó Ciardha, *Ireland and the Jacobite cause, 1685–1766: a fatal attachment* (2002), 122–4

Dunlap, John
1746/7–1812
Printer

John Dunlap was born in what is now Meetinghouse Street, Strabane, Co. Tyrone, a younger son among probably three sons and four daughters of John Dunlap, saddler, and Sarah Dunlap (née Ector). He may have been apprenticed to learn the printing trade in Gray's of Strabane; when he was about 10, he was sent to assist his uncle William Dunlap, who had earlier emigrated to America. William Dunlap had married Benjamin Franklin's niece, and was a printer and bookseller; Franklin appointed him postmaster of Philadelphia (1757), but in 1764 he was replaced by another Franklin relative. Partly as a result, William Dunlap got into financial difficulties. In 1766 he gave up bookselling to enter the ministry of the Church of England, and in 1768 John Dunlap, who had completed his apprenticeship, bought his uncle's printing business. He at first had to sleep under the counter in the printing shop. The following year he reprinted an English political satire and attributed it to Benjamin Franklin to increase sales.

In November 1771 Dunlap started a weekly newspaper, the *Pennsylvania Packet*; on 21 September 1784 it became the first newspaper of significance in America to be published daily. Around 1777 he was also publishing the *Maryland Gazette*. In 1774 Dunlap published a reprint of Thomas Jefferson's *Summary view of the rights of British America*; he was also official printer to the Continental Congress which met in Philadelphia. On 4 July 1776 that body formally adopted the Declaration of Independence, which was thereupon printed overnight by Dunlap for distribution to the colonial assemblies; surviving copies of this document are regarded as historical and bibliographical treasures of the United States. In September 1777, when Philadelphia was taken by the British, Dunlap moved his press to Lancaster, Pennsylvania, where he printed material for the revolutionary Pennsylvania assembly and also printed the journals of the Continental Congress. He was the first printer to re-establish business in Philadelphia in July 1778. Dunlap and his partner also printed the constitution of the United States in 1787.

Dunlap, one of the founders in 1774 of the 1st Troop of Philadelphia City Cavalry, saw active service as a cornet in the War of Independence in 1776–7; in 1780 he subscribed £4,000 to found the National Bank for the United States to provide supplies for the new country's army. He was a major in command of the cavalry during the Pennsylvania 'whiskey insurrection' of 1794. From 1789 to 1792 he was a member of the Common Council of Philadelphia. Dunlap helped several of his relations to emigrate from Ireland, was charitable and fair-minded, and somewhat intemperate. He retired in 1795 a very wealthy man; he had speculated in land, and owned 98,000 acres in several states. He married (4 February 1773) Elizabeth Ellison (née Hayes), a widow from Liverpool, and they had five daughters and three sons; two of the sons died in infancy. Dunlap died on 27 November 1812 of apoplexy while reading the newspaper, and was buried with military honours in the graveyard of Christ Church, Philadelphia.

Linde Lunney

SOURCES

DAB; George W. Corner (ed.), *The autobiography of Benjamin Rush: his travels through life together with his commonplace book for 1789–1813* (1948), 319; Leonard Labaree (ed.), *The papers of Benjamin Franklin,* xiii (1969), 84n; William B. Willcox (ed.), *The papers of Benjamin Franklin,* xvi (1972), 62; Frederick R. Goff, *The John Dunlap broadside: the first printing of the Declaration of Independence* (1976) (portrait, *c.* 1803); *ADB;* Public Record Office of Northern Ireland, Aug. 1998, material from internet website on the Dunlap papers (T1336); genealogical information extracted from Virgil D. White, *Genealogical abstracts of revolutionary war pension files* (1990–92) and from John T. Humphrey, *Pennsylvania births: Philadelphia county* (1994), supplied by Oscar Dunlap (family historian) of Texas; information from Ken Dunlap (family historian)

Embury, Philip
1728–73
Methodist preacher

Philip Embury was one of at least four sons and one daughter of Andreas Imberger (d. *c.* 1755), tenant farmer, a German Palatine immigrant of 1709. Philip was baptised (29 September 1728) a member of the Church of Ireland in Ballingrane, Co. Limerick. With his cousin Barbara Heck, Philip Embury has been credited with being one of the first properly documented founders of Methodism in America and chief instigator of the building of the first Wesleyan church in North America.

Tradition tells that Embury, a carpenter by trade, was educated in German within the Palatine community in Ballingrane and that he later attended an English school, probably in the town of Rathkeale. He may have first come in contact with John Wesley's teachings in 1749 when Philip Guier, the burgomaster of Ballingrane, established a Methodist society in his home village. Embury converted to Methodism (25 December 1752) and was licensed as a Methodist lay preacher in 1758, by which time a Methodist chapel had been erected in the centre of the village square at Courtmatrix, one of the three original Co. Limerick Palatine settlements near Rathkeale. Embury is reputed to have done the carpentry for this building.

He and his wife were among twenty-five or more young Palatines forming a company to set up a linen business in North America. In June 1760 they left Limerick for New York on board the *Pery* and arrived on 10 August. In New York the Emburys lived in Barrack Street and Philip worked as a teacher of reading, writing, and arithmetic (in English) while they petitioned for 25,000 acres of land on which he and his friends could set up their linen and hempen manufactory. The Emburys at first attended Trinity Lutheran Church, Rector Street (later Cliff Street), New York, where the first three of their children were baptised between 1761 and 1765. In 1766 the Emburys and others of the Irish Palatine community became members of the new Lutheran Christ Church, built on the corner of Frankfurt Street and William Street, where Embury and Barbara's husband, Paul Heck, appear on the list of original subscribers.

Between 1760 and 1765 Paul Heck's brothers Jacob and John and Barbara's brother, Paul Ruttle, arrived with some other Palatines from Co. Limerick, and tradition tells that Barbara was horrified when she came across the newcomers gambling at cards, and implored Embury to preach to them. He began preaching at first in his own home to his family and friends (1766) and then, as his congregation grew, he preached in the city barracks and in a sail-rigging loft on Horse and Cart Street. He is also known to have preached in the Poor House. From 1767 onwards another Irishman, half-pay officer Capt. Thomas Webb, assisted him. Dublin Methodists, Charles White and Richard Sause, joined them shortly afterwards. Embury and the other English and Irish Methodists raised subscriptions and in March 1768 purchased a lot in John Street, where they built a chapel, the design of which is said to have been drawn up by Barbara Heck who also, tradition says, whitewashed the interior. This was the first chapel in the world to be named after John Wesley. Embury is reputed to have constructed the pulpit, and he and Paul Heck also carried out other interior woodwork.

On 30 October 1768 he preached his first formal sermon there. The Emburys moved into an old Dutch-style house on the property, which was then used as a parsonage. In November 1769 Wesley sent preachers who formalised the situation and John Street chapel was transferred to Wesley's Methodist Connexion on 2 November 1770, six or seven months after Embury and his compatriots had moved to Camden Valley (present-day White Creek), Charlotte County, New York, where they had leased land from a prominent lawyer of Irish descent. Embury was appointed JP for Albany County (1770) and for Charlotte County (1772). He was also appointed one of the commissioners of roads for Charlotte County. Embury and a fellow Methodist, Thomas Ashton, formed a Methodist Society at Ashgrove and a class at West Camden (1770). For the next three years he continued to preach, sometimes travelling to outlying areas to do so. He died of pleurisy in August 1773, leaving a wife and four children, and is buried in Woodland cemetery, Cambridge, New York. His oldest son Samuel later became a local Methodist preacher in Upper Canada.

Embury married (31 October 1758) in the Church of Ireland, Rathkeale, Co. Limerick, Margaret (1743–1807), one of eight children and only surviving daughter of Christopher and Elizabeth Switzer, Palatine tenant farmers of Courtmatrix. Their children were Catherine Elizabeth (1761–2), John Albert (1762–6), Samuel (1765–1853), Catherine (c. 1767–1831), Anna (c. 1769–1775), and Philip (1772–5). There are portraits of Philip and Margaret Embury dated 1773 at John Street United Methodist Church, New York City.

Vivien Hick

SOURCES
J. B. Wakeley, *Lost chapters recovered from the early history of American Methodism* (1858); Samuel J. Fanning, 'Philip Embury, founder of Methodism in New York', *Methodist History*, iii (1965), 16–25; Eula C. Lapp, *To their heirs forever* (1977); Arthur Bruce Moss, 'Philip Embury's preaching mission at Chesterfield, New Hampshire', *Methodist History*, xvi (1978), 101–09; id., 'Philip Embury's Bible', *Methodist History*, xvii (1979), 253–60

Finley, Samuel
1715–66
Presbyterian minister and principal of Princeton

Samuel Finley was one of seven pious brothers born in Co. Armagh. Some genealogies state that his parents were Michael Finley and Ann Finley (née O'Neill) of Mullaghbrack, Co. Armagh, and that he was born on 2 July 1715, but this information is not conclusively attested. Samuel received a good education in Ireland; from the age of six, when he first heard a sermon, he intended to become a minister. He emigrated to America, arriving in Philadelphia on 28 September 1734, and was probably a student for several years in the celebrated 'log college' of William Tennent (1673–1746). In August 1740 he was licensed by the New Brunswick presbytery to preach, and on 13 October 1742 was ordained. He was influenced by George Whiteside and by William Tennent (1705–77) and Gilbert Tennent, evangelical preachers who insisted on the validity of personal salvation, and he took a vigorous part in the controversies that followed the 'Great Awakening'; he published polemic sermons and pamphlets in support of the doctrines and tenets of the Calvinistic 'New Side'. He also attacked the Baptists' beliefs in two tracts (1746, 1748).

Finley travelled widely in New Jersey, Pennsylvania, and Connecticut; in the latter state the authorities chose to regard him as a vagrant since the church to which he was travelling had no legal status, and he was briefly imprisoned in 1743 and then deported from the state. In 1744 he accepted a call to the congregation of Nottingham, on the border between Maryland and Pennsylvania, and there established a school which enjoyed a considerable reputation in his own day, and which survives (in 2019) as West Nottingham Academy, one of the two oldest boarding schools in America. The students lived in Finley's household, and he insisted that all should experience farmwork as well as gaining experience in 'the common forms of good breeding' (*Rush*, 26). He displayed 'apostolic prudence, piety and zeal' (ibid., 33) and was so much beloved that after his death some of his pupils expressed their respect for his memory in 'terms bordering upon idolatry' (ibid., 190). In 1761 he was unanimously elected principal of the College of New Jersey, better known as Princeton.

Finley corresponded with ministers in America and elsewhere; he was the first American Presbyterian minister to be awarded an honorary degree by a European university when Glasgow awarded him a DD (1763). Princeton flourished under Finley's guidance; enrolment increased, and he planted trees, some of which survive. In 1766 he went to Philadelphia to seek medical advice; he died there on 17 July 1766, after a painful illness. His conduct on his deathbed was so edifying that an attendant's description of his last days was published in the *United States Magazine*, i (1794). Eight members of Princeton's senior class travelled to Philadelphia to be his pallbearers; he was buried in the Second Presbyterian Church, beside his friend Gilbert Tennent. Finley married first Sarah Hall (d. 1760), whose nephew Benjamin Rush was a pupil in Nottingham. Rush showed his gratitude to the family by adopting and educating the youngest of Finley's eight children, a son who was the only one that lived till after 1789. Finley married secondly (1761) Anna Clarkson, probably the sister of one of his pupils. They seem not to have had children. John Finley, a notable pioneer who is said to have shown Daniel Boone the way into what later became Kentucky, may have been Samuel Finley's nephew. Samuel Finley Breese Morse, who developed the telegraph, was a great-grandson of Samuel Finley, and in 1870 presented a portrait of his ancestor to Princeton.

Linde Lunney

SOURCES
Appleton; *DAB*; Thomas Jefferson Wertenbaker, *Princeton 1746–1896* (1946, repr. 1976), 24, 27, 45, 102; George W. Corner (ed.), *The autobiography of Benjamin Rush: his travels through life, together with his commonplace book for 1789–1813* (1948), 26, 33, 190; David B. Calhoun, *Princeton seminary*, i (1994), 9–10; *Blackwell dictionary of evangelical biography 1730–1860*, i (1995); *ANB*; West Nottingham Academy website, http://www.wna.org/NewWebPage/webimages/subpages/aboutwna.htm#History (portr.); 'Samuel Finley' at http://etc/princeton.edu/CampusWWW/Companion/finley_samuel.html; genealogical information at http://www.kittybrewster.com/shadow/finley.htm (all accessed June 2004)

Fitzsimons, Thomas
1741–1811
Merchant and politician

Thomas Fitzsimons (Fitzsimmons) was born in Ireland, probably as a younger son, and seems to have had at least three brothers and a twin sister. His birthplace is variously given as Nobber, Co. Wicklow; Limerick; the north of Ireland; and Edenderry (Co. Offaly or Co. Antrim or Co. Down). The family emigrated to America before 1760; Thomas, who had received a passable education in Ireland, became a clerk in a merchant's office in Philadelphia. On 28 November 1761 he married Catherine, daughter of Robert Meade, who had become a wealthy merchant after emigrating from Co. Limerick. Both families were Catholic. Fitzsimons went into business with George Meade, his brother-in-law; he was a partner from 1771, and prospered in the West Indies trade. After America declared its independence from Britain, Catholics were able for the first time to be involved in local politics; Fitzsimons became a member of the Philadelphia council of safety and naval board and supervised the building of fire ships to protect the port. His company was involved with privateering, and gave $5,000 to provide supplies for the Continental army. In command of a militia company he saw some active service in New Jersey during the War of Independence; he was a delegate from Pennsylvania to the Continental Congress in 1782–3. He strongly supported plans to redeem the public debt; troops who had not been paid threatened the Congress in June 1783, and it moved to the safety of Princeton. On 20 November 1783 a meeting at Fitzsimons's lodgings proposed a compromise on tax collection, which was subsequently adopted.

He served several terms in the state legislature, and was one of those who worked for years in support of the new, less radical state constitution that was adopted in 1790. Fitzsimons was also a member of the convention that prepared the federal constitution of 1787; he was a supporter of Alexander Hamilton's federalist position, and on occasion expressed his views on commercial matters. He favoured a strong central government, a property-based franchise, and federal taxation. He was elected to the new Congress in 1788, and again represented his state in 1790 and 1792; still opposing the continued existence of a national debt, and advocating a protectionist tariff, he was a prominent member of the ad hoc congressional ways and means committee (1789), and was a commissioner to implement some of the commercial provisions of Jay's treaty of 1794. He lost the election of 1794, but remained active in public life as a trustee of the University of Pennsylvania, as a philanthropist in Catholic affairs in Philadelphia, as president of the Philadelphia chamber of commerce (1805), and in the Friendly Sons of St Patrick. His contribution to public education is commemorated in the name of a school in downtown Philadelphia. Fitzsimons was one of the founders (1781) of the first bank in the USA, the Bank of North America; he was a director until 1803. He was also a founder and for many years a director of the Insurance Company of North America. He was heartbroken when ambitious speculations in western land, entered into on behalf of his long-time friend Robert Morris, went spectacularly wrong, and he became a bankrupt in 1805; he regained some of his wealth, and at his death (on 26 August 1811) was regarded with respect and gratitude by his fellow citizens. He was buried in St Mary's churchyard, Philadelphia, beside his wife, who died on 20 June 1810. They had no children.

Linde Lunney

SOURCES

DAB; Richard J. Purcell, 'Thomas Fitzsimons, framer of the American constitution', *Studies: an Irish Quarterly Review*, xxvii (1938), 273–90; George W. Corner (ed.), *The autobiography of Benjamin Rush: his travels through life, together with his commonplace book for 1789–1813* (1948), 178, 318; E. James Ferguson, *The power of the purse: a history of American public finance 1776–1790* (1961), 166; Harold C. Syrett (ed.), *The papers of Alexander Hamilton* (27 vols, 1961–87); Richard G. Miller, *Philadelphia, the federalist city: a study of urban politics 1789–1801* (1976); James Hennessy, *American Catholics: a history of the Roman Catholic community in the United States* (1981), 59; *ANB*; material from US House of Representatives Committee Office Web Services (accessed Oct. 1998)

Gaine, Hugh
1726–1807
Printer and newspaper editor in New York

Hugh Gaine was born in Portglenone, Co. Antrim, the son of Hugh Gaine, possibly a merchant. There was at least one other son, who also emigrated. The family was Church of Ireland, although in a 1766 religious census family members registered as both Dissenters and Anglicans. The Gaines were clearly prosperous: on 17 December 1740, the father paid £100 for his son's apprenticeship to James Magee and Samuel Wilson, who were in partnership as printers in Belfast. When the partnership was dissolved in 1744, the apprenticeship ended a year early, but Gaine emigrated to New York and became a journeyman printer with James Parker.

From 1752 Gaine had his own printing business, the Bible and Crown, and was increasingly successful. He moved twice to larger premises, printing several almanacs annually and other books, as well as blank forms, and selling all kinds of goods: stationery, cloth, tobacco, razors and even Irish butter and patent medicines. In August 1752 he published a newspaper, the *New-York Mercury* (from 1768 the *New-York Gazette and Weekly Mercury*), which at first contained mainly advertisements and anodyne local news items, as well as foreign and shipping intelligence. A row in 1753 with prominent Presbyterians in the town, over his refusal to print a letter on the Anglican influence over plans for King's College (latterly, Columbia University), was Gaine's first experience of controversy, as both sides subsequently published defences of their views.

Even in this early phase, Gaine's claimed impartiality was motivated more by concern for his business than by any strongly held ideals about the freedom of the press. In general, Gaine saw events from an Anglican and establishment viewpoint, but he came to an agreement with the Presbyterians and published their material for several years, even though some of it was of a whiggish and even radical cast. In 1768 he became official printer for the colony of New York, and from 1769 to 1775 for both the colony and city of New York, making him still less likely to risk offending the authorities. His printing of large and complex volumes of the votes and legislation passed by the New York assembly more or less fully occupied his workshop during 1762–4 and 1774.

For a time Gaine made common cause with colonial whigs and radicals, particularly (like many other printers) in opposing the notorious stamp act of 1765, which threatened his business interests by applying a tax on paper used for printing legal documents, newspapers and books. In 1768 his newspaper criticised British military reprisals against rioting Bostonians, and as late as 1773 he printed public announcements of the radical Sons of Liberty. By that date, however, the merchant's instinctive fear of the mob, along with the Anglican's respect for the crown's authority, were more important in forming his attitudes. When the taxes, except for the tax on tea, were repealed, the *New-York Gazette* called in 1773 for an end to protests. As demonstrations and rioting spread through the colonies, Gaine reported them selectively, leading some within the emergent patriot party to accuse him of failing to support their cause.

In September 1776, when invasion of the city by the British army was imminent, Gaine fled with some printing equipment to Newark, New Jersey. Matters looked bleak that autumn for the Continental army and its supporters, however, and Gaine seems to have decided to make his peace with the British authorities, returning to his New York office in November 1776.

As a result of Gaine's divided loyalties, the colonial authorities did not trust him, and an English-born rival was made king's printer. On the other side, former allies now identifying as patriots regarded him as a 'trimmer' or even a traitor. Gaine was fortunate that his ambivalence had no lasting serious consequences; though privately he seems to have held loyalist views throughout, his overt allegiance to the crown disappeared after the ending of British rule. He took care to limit political news in the *Gazette*, and from 1783, after thirty-one years, discontinued the publication. The word 'Crown' was dropped from the company name after 1780. Gaine's newspapers, annual *Universal Register*, public statements, and journals (available for several years around 1770) are important sources of information on the course of the revolution and its aftermath, and important examples of the complexities of attitudes in such epochs. Not all Ulster-born emigrants were on the patriot side; not everyone kept a straight course through the events of rebellion and war.

Gaine's business acumen, personal qualities and reputation for honesty preserved his wealth and his various enterprises through the stormy times following the revolution. He continued to print books until 1800, and was still one of New York's most important booksellers in 1802. In 1792 he printed a catalogue of his stock, over 500 items, an impressively representative list of contemporary works. He was appointed to print the laws and statutes of the city of New York in 1784. Despite the huge output of books, almanacs and newspapers, Gaine's work as a printer was generally regarded by contemporaries as competent rather than ground-breaking. Among his more innovative ventures was the printing for Sir William Johnson of an edition of the Book of Common Prayer in the Mohawk language (1769). The printing of Bibles, prayer books and other religious material formed an important part of Gaine's business; he was a vestryman in Trinity Church, where Charles Inglis was then assistant rector.

Gaine was also involved in many other businesses. He and two partners (Dutch loyalists) established a paper mill in 1773 at Hempstead Harbor, Long Island, and afterwards sold paper of all sorts in his shop in Hanover Square. He owned other property in New York and developed his holdings as the town expanded northwards after the revolution, on occasion being involved in paving streets. He built a large country residence on the King's Bridge Road, and was one of the twenty-eight speculators who in 1770 purchased 28,000 acres of land in Albany county, along the Susquehanna river; the estate was known as the Wallace Land Patent after two of the main partners, the brothers Hugh (d. 1788) and Alexander (d. 1800) Wallace, wealthy Waterford-born merchants and uncompromising loyalists, who returned to Ireland after the revolution.

In public life Gaine played a significant but not showy role; he was a freemason and in 1754 a founding member of New York Society Library. When this was revived in 1788, he was a trustee. He was also vice-president of the New York Hospital, and in 1802 was instrumental in forming a trade association of American booksellers, along with Matthew Carey of Philadelphia. Gaine was its first president. He was so well known in New York, and so well regarded, that he was frequently asked to witness legal documents and to act as executor in wills. It is in this regard that his name appears in the letters of the Irish political activist William Drennan and his sister Martha McTier. For years Drennan and McTier were involved in efforts to profit from the will of Hamilton Young (d. 1799), their cousin and one of Gaine's partners in the Wallace Land Patent. The will was said to be in Gaine's possession, but Alexander Wallace, a distant relative of Young's, claimed to be the beneficiary by another will. Discussion of the complicated legal wranglings occupied many pages of the Drennan-McTier correspondence.

Gaine married (24 October 1759) Sarah Robbins. They had two daughters and a son before Sarah died in 1765. Gaine married secondly (5 September 1769) Cornelia Wallace (née van Dam), of a well-known Dutch family. Her grandfather was Rip van Dam, who had briefly been governor of New York (1731–2), and her first husband was John Wallace, possibly a brother or other relative of the Waterford Wallaces, Gaine's business partners. Hugh and Cornelia had two daughters. In 1791 the household included five slaves.

Hugh Gaine's son died before him, but when Hugh himself died, on 25 April 1807, he was able to leave a large fortune to his widow and daughters, and had more or less outlived his reputation as a turncoat. If it were not for an amusing and even affectionate poem, 'Hugh Gaine's life' (1783), by the noted poet of the revolution, Philip Freneau, partisan historians would have had fewer witty quotations with which to try to blacken Gaine's name.

Linde Lunney

SOURCES
Hugh Gaine papers, New York Public Library, digital collections, digitalcollections.nypl.org; Paul Leicester Ford (ed.), *The journals of Hugh Gaine, printer* (1902), full text available on archive.org; Alfred Lawrence Lorenz, *Hugh Gaine: a colonial printer-editor's odyssey to loyalism* (1972); Timothy M. Barnes, *Loyalist newspapers of the American revolution, 1763–1783: a bibliography* (1974); Thomas M. Truxes, *Irish-American trade 1660–1783* (1988), 115; *ANB*; Jean Agnew (ed.), *The Drennan-McTier letters* (1999), vols. ii and iii, *passim*; Ronald 'Ron' Baldwin, 'The Wallace Land Patent of 1770' (3 Mar. 2005), threerivershms.com/wallace1770.htm; John Bidwell, *American paper mills, 1690–1832: a directory of the paper trade …* (2013); internet material accessed Aug.–Sept. 2017

Grant, Jasper
1762–1812
Army officer in Canada and collector of ethnographical material

Jasper Grant was second son of Thomas Grant, gentleman, of Kilmurry, Co. Cork, and his wife Elizabeth, daughter of Thomas Campion of Co. Leitrim. His elder brother, Thomas Grant, inherited the family estate; his younger brother was the Rev. Alexander Grant, vicar of Clondulane. Jasper was educated by private tutor and was commissioned as an ensign in the 4th Foot in 1781. Shortly afterwards he transferred into the 70th Foot and exchanged into the 41st Foot in 1793, with the rank of major. He took part in the 1796–7 campaign by Gen. Ralph Abercromby in the West Indies, during the course of which the army was decimated by yellow fever. The 41st Foot suffered heavily; soon there were only eight officers remaining, and Grant took command of the battalion.

He returned to Ireland at the end of the campaign and, some time between 1797 and 1799, married Isabella ('Bell') Odell. In 1800 he was posted to Canada with the 41st Foot and Isabella decided to accompany him with their young son, Jasper Grant, jr. He was initially posted to

Quebec before being appointed in 1802 as commanding officer at Fort George near Niagara. Here he met for the first time native peoples, mostly Iroquois and Ojibwa, and his letters home mention his dealings with them and also the forbidding nature of the territory. From 1803 to 1805 he served again in Quebec before returning to Fort George, where he remained in command until 1806.

In 1806 he was given command of Fort Malden at Amhertsburg on the Great Lakes, an important centre of the fur trade. His new posting was not only remote but was also in the middle of the homeland of various indigenous peoples. These included Ottawas, Hurons, Chippewas, and Potawantomis; he was responsible for maintaining the alliances that had been formed with these tribes, and every summer there was a great gathering of tribes at Amhertsburg. During this gathering he gave the tribal chiefs presents, ensuring their loyalty to the British. It was customary for them to give him gifts also, and in 1806 alone 4,443 Native Americans visited the fort. These included Chippewas, Shawnees, Ottawas, Delawares, Mingoes (Ohio Senecas), Cherokees, Miamis, and Mohawks. He displayed considerable diplomatic skill and fostered good relations with indigenous peoples throughout this period, much to the discontent of the governors of the northern American states. His alliances with native chiefs were especially important as war with America seemed likely in 1807–08, and Grant became responsible for organising Britain's native allies into large war bands.

During his career in Canada he gathered a large collection of native material. Indeed he was an avid collector, not only of tribal pieces, but also of botanical and zoological specimens. It is also likely that his wife, Isabella, played an important part in the creation of this collection; she mentioned it as a separate item in her will, referring to it as her 'Indian cabinet'. The collection is large, containing fifty-nine items; it is also one of the best-documented 'first contact' collections of First Nations material in the world, and includes extremely delicate items such as decorated deerskin shirts and leggings. The Grants also collected sashes, armbands, and garter pendants. Wooden items, such as war clubs, pipes, and utensils were included, and there is a small number of pieces of wampum beadwork. There are some early examples of 'souvenir art' – pieces made especially for soldiers and traders living in the area. When he left Amhertsburg in 1809, ten local chiefs presented him with a gift of wampum and an illuminated address.

In the course of his duties he attended many tribal meetings and made copies of speeches. It is possible that he met the great Native American leader Tecumseh, as his papers contain a copy of one of Tecumseh's speeches. His opinion of the natives themselves seems to have varied greatly but by the end of his time in Canada he would appear to have become captivated by them and was also aware of the negative aspect for them of contact with Europeans. In a letter to his brother he wrote: 'The more removed Indians are from all intercourse with white people, the more cleanly in their persons and moral in their characters they are' (Bliss, 19). Apart from the First Nations material, Grant also collected cuttings of plants, which he sent home to Cork to be planted on his estate. He sent home zoological specimens and even a live squirrel to his nephew, who kept it for many years as a pet.

Jasper Grant in 1809 returned to Ireland, where he sought appointment to a government post. Eventually he succeeded in being appointed deputy lieutenant of Co. Carlow but died soon afterwards on 5 March 1812 at Lismore, Co. Waterford. Isabella lived until 9 June 1855, and passed the collection on to her two daughters, though her will was disputed. Her grandson, Robert Ussher, presented the collection to the National Museum of Ireland in 1902. It had been lovingly preserved over the years and it has been recognised internationally as an important collection. In 1985 it was included as part of a major exhibition of First Nations art and material culture and was displayed at a number of venues in Canada and America. The Grant letter collection is held in the National Library of Ireland.

David Murphy

SOURCES
NLI, MSS 10177, 10178 (Ussher papers), letters of Col. Jasper Grant; *Waterford Mail*, 8 July 1856; Ruth B. Bliss, *Patterns of power* (1984); information from Dr Bill Rawlings, National Military Archives of Canada, and Rachel Hand, ethnographical section, NMI

Heck, Barbara
1734–1804
Methodist

Barbara Heck was born in Ballingrane, Co. Limerick, daughter of Sebastian Ruckle (surname later found also as Ruttle), tenant farmer on the Southwell estate, and his wife Margaret (née Embury). The Ruckles, Emburys, and Hecks were part of a group of Rhineland immigrants, popularly known as Palatines, who settled in Ireland in 1709. Barbara was literate in English and her early education probably took place in Ballingrane. With her cousin Philip Embury, Heck has been credited with being among the first properly documented founders of Methodism in America and architects of one of the first Methodist churches in North America. Unfortunately there are few surviving primary sources, and most of what we know of her comes from Methodist tradition.

Known to later generations of Methodists as the 'Mother of Methodism', she converted in 1752. In June 1760 she and her husband, Paul Heck, were among twenty-five or more young Palatines to leave Limerick on board the *Pery*, arriving in New York on 10 August. The Hecks at first attended Trinity Lutheran Church in New York, where the first three of their children were baptised. Barbara is credited with inspiring Philip Embury's return to preaching after she came on some of the Palatine men gambling at cards. Embury began preaching at first in his own home to his family and friends (1766), then, as his congregation grew, he preached in the city barracks and in a sail-rigging loft on Horse and Cart Street In March 1768 Embury and other English and Irish Methodists purchased a lot in John Street, where they built a chapel, the design of which is attributed to Barbara Heck (who, tradition says, also whitewashed the interior). This was the first chapel in the world to be named after John Wesley, and it was here on 30 October 1768 that Embury preached his first formal sermon. After 1769 Wesley sent preachers who regularised the situation, and on 2 November 1770 John Street chapel was transferred to Wesley's Methodist Connexion. In the spring of 1770 Heck, Embury, and other members of the Palatine group moved to Camden Valley, Charlotte County, New York, where they leased land from lawyer James Duane. Heck appears to have assisted Embury in his ministry up until his death (1773) and is known to have set up at least one Methodist class meeting (in the town of Hampton).

When the revolution reached their homes many of the Palatine men, including Paul Heck, joined the loyalist forces, where they formed part of the King's Royal Regiment of New York under Capt. Robert Leake. The Palatine farms in the Camden valley were, in consequence, confiscated in 1778 and the women and children fled to Canada. By way of compensation the Palatine loyalists were eventually granted land by the British government in township no. 7, 3rd concession (Augusta), Upper Canada (1785). The Hecks and other Palatines who settled in the Bay of Quinte area helped found the Augusta Methodist Society, which formed the nucleus of one of the first circuits of what later became the Canada conference of the Methodist Episcopal Church.

Barbara Heck died on 17 August 1804, at her son's home in the hamlet of Maynard, Augusta township, in present-day Ontario, Canada. She is buried in the Blue Church cemetery, Prescott, Ontario.

She married (1760) Paul Heck (1730–95), son of John Heck, tenant farmer, in Ballingrane, Co. Limerick. They had seven children, three of whom survived to adulthood. Their son Samuel (1771–1844) was baptised in Arlington (in present-day Vermont) in a group baptism with seven other Palatine children on 4 February 1774 by the Rev. Gideon Bostwick of Great Barrington, Massachusetts; Samuel Heck became a local preacher in Augusta in 1803, and was ordained deacon 1817 and elder 1828. Their other children were Jacobina Elizabeth (b. 1761, died young), Catherine Barbara (died at birth, 1763), Elizabeth Maria (b. 1765); John (1767–1805); Jacob (1769–1847); and Nancy (1772–c. 1781).

Barbara Heck's portrait can be found at the United Library, Garret-Evangelical and Seabury-Western Theological Seminaries, Evanston, Ill., USA. Heck and Embury family papers are in the Archives and History Centre of the United Methodist Church, Drew University, Madison, NJ, USA. The records of John Street church are in the manuscript and archives section, New York Public Library.

Vivien Hick

SOURCES

William Crook, *Ireland and the centenary of American Methodism* (1866); Abel Stevens, *The women of Methodism: its three foundresses* (1866); Ruthella Mary Bibbins, *How Methodism came: the beginnings of Methodism in America* (1945; repr. 1987); Frank Baker, *From Wesley to Ashbury: studies in early American Methodism* (1976); Eula C. Lapp, *To their heirs forever* (1977); Carolyn A. Heald, 'Barbara Heck: the mother of North American Methodism in symbol and myth' (paper for graduate seminar at Queen's Univ., Kingston, Ontario, 1993)

Hemphill, Samuel
fl. 1729–35
Presbyterian minister

Samuel Hemphill was born *c.* 1705 and educated at the University of Glasgow. He was licensed to preach by Strabane presbytery in 1729/30, having subscribed the Westminster confession, and was ordained to minister in America. He and Patrick Vance, an older man who was minister in Ray, Co. Donegal, preached on the same text of Scripture and disagreed on its interpretation. Vance subsequently accused Hemphill of unsound doctrine, and in a letter to his brother-in-law in America he described Hemphill as an 'eminent instrument of the devil', whose preaching would work mischief in the infant American church (*Records of the general synod*). Though he later publicly withdrew the accusation, the matter was raised in the general synod in 1735, a year after Hemphill (furnished with a recommendation from Strabane presbytery and all necessary certificates) travelled to America.

A controversy there over the requirement to subscribe the Westminster confession had just subsided; Hemphill subscribed as required, and was accordingly accepted by the synod of Philadelphia. Doubts about his orthodoxy, encouraged by the circulation of Vance's letter, were again expressed after he preached in New London, Pennsylvania, but he became assistant minister to the elderly Jedediah Andrews in Philadelphia. The new minister's sermons attracted large congregations, some from other churches, and Benjamin Franklin was one of those who heard him with approval. Other, more Calvinist, congregational members boycotted the church, and on 7 April 1735, at a meeting of synod, Andrews brought formal charges of erroneous preaching against his assistant. Three days later Benjamin Franklin published in his paper, the *Pennsylvania Gazette*, a 'Dialogue between two Presbyterians' in which he defended the young minister. Hemphill regarded the commission of synod that tried his case from 17 April 1735 as biased against him; he was found guilty of 'unsound and dangerous' preaching (quoted in Le Beau). He was suspended from the ministry pending a meeting of synod in September 1735.

Franklin again intervened in July 1735 with a published critique of the conduct of the trial, and defended Hemphill's principles and theology. During the summer Hemphill's opponents claimed to have detected numerous plagiarisms from English deist authors in his sermons, proving to their satisfaction both his lack of veracity and his non-Presbyterian theology. On 22 September 1735 Hemphill's letter was read to the synod; in it, he refused to appear before them, and in a postscript added: 'I shall think you will do me a deal of honor, if you entirely excommunicate me' (quoted in Le Beau). The same day appeared Hemphill's *A letter to a friend in the country* ..., with a preface by Franklin; both argued against the church authorities' reliance on subscription and claim to be allowed to examine ministers. Franklin's attack on 'a smug and tyrannical clergy which denies truth to itself and to others' (ibid.) most certainly did not help Hemphill's position with the synod, but the minister's own attitude and resort to public comment on his case was decisive: Hemphill was unanimously judged 'unqualified for any future exercise of his ministry' (ibid.) within the jurisdiction of the synod of Philadelphia. Franklin's *Defense of the Reverend Hemphill's observations* in October 1735 again trenchantly attacked the church establishment, and as in all his writings in the controversy, explored concepts increasingly central to his own thought, such as individual liberty of conscience and the reasonableness of the Christian religion.

To some extent, Hemphill was for Franklin a stalking horse, and the young minister was perhaps unfortunate that Franklin decided to support him. Hemphill's implacable adversaries branded him a contumacious plagiarist; the church authorities in Philadelphia thereafter tightened their control on the admission of candidates for the ministry, particularly those coming from the north of Ireland, and Franklin abandoned the Presbyterian church. Nothing is known of Hemphill's subsequent career, but he could never have served as a minister again.

Linde Lunney

SOURCES

James Seaton Reid, *History of the Presbyterian Church in Ireland*, iii (1867), 204; Thomas Witherow, *Historical and literary memorials of Presbyterianism in Ireland*, (1880), 250–51; *Records of the General Synod of Ulster, from 1691–1820*, ii (1897), 149, 208–9; Guy S. Klett, *Presbyterians in colonial Pennsylvania* (1937), 143–5; McConnell, *Fasti*; Leonard W. Labaree (ed.), *The papers of Benjamin Franklin*, ii (1960), 27–9, 37–49, 90–91; A. W. Godfrey Brown, 'A theological interpretation of the first subscription controversy (1719–1728)', J. M. Haire (ed.), *Challenge and conflict: essays in Irish Presbyterian history and doctrine* (1981); *A history of congregations in the Presbyterian Church in Ireland 1610–1982* (1982), 56, 280; Bryan Le Beau, 'Franklin and the Presbyterians; freedom of conscience versus the need for order', *Early America Review* (summer 1996), unpaginated, http://earlyamerica.com/review/summer/franklin/ (downloaded Sept. 2004); information from Robert Hemphill, family historian, via Genforum

Holmes, William
1663–1746
Presbyterian minister

William Holmes (Homes) was born in Donaghmore, Co. Donegal, of a family well established in Donegal and Co. Tyrone and probably originating in the Salisbury area of Wiltshire. His father was probably Robert Holmes, who was an elder in Donaghmore after 1672, and he had at least one brother (killed by lightning in 1692) and at least one sister. He received a good education; in about 1689 he travelled to America and was a teacher on the island of Martha's Vineyard, Massachusetts, for three years. He returned to Ireland in July 1691 to study for the ministry of the Presbyterian church; on 21 December 1692 he was ordained minister in the congregation of Strabane. On 26 September 1693 he married Katherine (d. 1754), daughter of the redoubtable Rev. Robert Craighead (Craghead) of Donaghmore and later of Derry; her brothers Thomas and Robert were also Presbyterian ministers.

Though known as 'Holmes the meek' to distinguish him from his cousin William Holmes who was a minister at the same time in the neighbouring congregation of Urney, Holmes's leadership qualities were recognised when he was chosen moderator of the general synod in 1703. In 1714 Holmes, his brother-in-law Thomas Craghead, and their families travelled to America; they arrived in Boston in the first week of October 1714. Holmes was well received by local church leaders and by Judge Samuel Sewall, who entertained him and sent him a present of turnips. Holmes returned in September 1715 to Martha's Vineyard as congregational minister of Chilmark. He may have been a member of the Charitable Irish Society of Boston in 1740. He published a sermon, as well as works on church government, prayer, and Scripture reading; his *Good government of Christian families* was published in 1747 as a memorial to him. He preferred the Presbyterian system to that of the Congregational churches in New England. His manuscript diary, a valuable source of local historical information, is preserved in the New England Historical Society library. He remained in Chilmark till his death on 17/20 June 1746.

It seems from William Holmes's journal that he was kept informed of discussions that his son Robert Homes, a sea captain, apparently had with the influential Bostonian clergyman Cotton Mather and with Massachusetts landowners prior to the arrival in summer and autumn 1718 of many Presbyterian emigrants under the leadership of James McGregor and others. According to a nineteenth-century historian of McGregor's settlement of Londonderry in New Hampshire, Robert Homes carried information about America back to Ireland, especially to the Presbyterians in Tyrone and Londonderry, encouraging them for the first time to consider emigration. It seems likely that William Holmes's wide kinship network and his standing in the Presbyterian community in the north of Ireland enabled him to transmit first-hand information about life in America, both before he left Ireland in 1714 and later through the agency of his son, and they may thus have influenced the decision of hundreds or even thousands of Ulster-Scots to leave Ireland for new opportunities in America. Over the next twenty years, many made the journey in ships captained by Robert Homes; in October 1718 his ship, full of passengers from Ireland, arrived in Boston.

Robert Homes (Holmes) (1694–*a.* 1743) was born on 23 July 1694 in Stragullin, Co. Tyrone; he was the eldest among two sons and seven daughters who accompanied their parents to America; another son died young in Ireland, but the other children married into locally prominent families. Robert married (3 April 1716) Mary Franklin of Boston, sister of Benjamin Franklin. They had two sons and a daughter; Mary Franklin Homes died of breast cancer in 1731, and Robert Homes died at sea before 1743.

Linde Lunney

SOURCES
Appletons; Alexander Lecky, *In the days of the Laggan Presbytery* (1908), app.; David Stewart, *Fasti of the American Presbyterian Church* (1943); McConnell, *Fasti*; Leonard W. Labaree (ed.), *The papers of Benjamin Franklin*, i (1960), p. lix; R. J. Dickson, *Ulster emigration to colonial America 1718–1775* (1966), 22; Charles K. Bolton, *Scotch-Irish pioneers in Ulster and America* (1910; repr. 1967), *passim*; information from Ed Cooper, family historian, via Genforum on the internet, Sept. 2000; information from Simon Elliott of Westmorland, England, collateral descendant of the Rev. William Holmes

Inglis, Charles
1734–1816
Clergyman and loyalist in America

Charles Inglis was born at Glencolumbkille, Co. Donegal, youngest of three sons of the Rev. Archibald Inglis, clergyman at Glen and Kilcar. Orphaned at the age of eleven, he was prevented by lack of money from entering Trinity College Dublin (though his older brother did), and instead Charles decided to emigrate to America around 1754. Arriving in Pennsylvania, he was employed as an assistant master at the Free School in Lancaster (1755–8). After a period of spiritual reflection, he travelled to England and was ordained an Anglican minister in London in 1758. Immediately he returned to America, as a missionary for the Society for the Propagation of the Gospel in Dover, Delaware, with jurisdiction over the whole of Kent County.

A charismatic preacher, Inglis soon doubled the numbers of his parishioners, and was unique in allowing black slaves to receive communion. He married (1764) Mary Vining, and this gave him connections to one of the most powerful families in Delaware; however, she died in childbirth shortly afterwards. Because of his evangelical zeal and preaching abilities he was appointed assistant rector in New York in 1765, the most prestigious parish in the colonies, under Samuel Auchmuty. While in New York he embarked on a period of self-education, learning Hebrew, Syriac, and Aramaic, and improving his Greek and Latin; in recognition of his scholarly prowess he was awarded a doctorate in divinity by Oxford University in 1778. He published his only theological work, an 180-page essay defending infant baptism, in 1768. After visiting the Mohawk valley in 1770 he became committed to converting the Native Americans, and urged the Church of England to establish itself in the wilderness. With the outbreak of war between the colonies and Britain (1775), he threw himself enthusiastically into polemical defences of the crown's position.

In total he published about thirty pamphlets and articles, most of them anonymously; the most famous and controversial was *The true interest of America impartially stated* (1776), a trenchant attack on Thomas Paine's *Common sense.* It speculated that France would side with Britain against the colonists, urged the Americans to avoid a declaration of independence, and suggested that a republican form of government would neither suit the country nor the people. However, almost all the copies were burned by the hangman and it made little impact. He helped save St Paul's from the great fire on 21 September 1776 and became rector of Trinity church after the death of Auchmuty the following year. In 1776 he played a leading role in defending loyalist interests in New York, even after its occupation by the

American army. He courageously continued to preach against the rebellion, and pray for the king, despite much opposition and many threats to his life. In 1783 he left the newly established USA and returned to Britain.

His vast colonial experience was much respected and on 12 August 1787 he was named first colonial bishop of Nova Scotia, with jurisdiction over Canada; this marked the beginning of one of the most successful periods of his life. Between 1787 and 1816 he founded forty-four churches in the region, and was also involved in the establishment of King's College at Windsor, Nova Scotia. He died on 24 February 1816 at his home near the parish church of Aylesford, after years of suffering from gout and malaria. He had married for the second time (31 May 1773) Margaret Crooke (d. 1783); they had two sons and two daughters. His son, John (c. 1781–1850), became the third bishop of Nova Scotia in 1825.

Patrick M. Geoghegan

SOURCES
'Relations between the Vermont separatists and Great Britain, 1789-91' (in Documents), *American Historical Review*, xxi (1916), 547–60; R. W. Jackson, *Charles Inglis of Glencolumbkille* (1962); Roger J. Champagne, 'New York's radicals and the coming of independence', *Journal of American History*, li (1964), 21–40; Elizabeth I. Nybakken, 'New light on the old side: Irish influences on colonial presbyterianism', *Journal of American History*, lxviii (1982), 813–32; Brian Cuthbertson, *The first bishop: a biography of Charles Inglis* (1987); *ANB*

Irvine, William
1741–1804
General in the American army

William Irvine was born on 3 November 1741 in Co. Fermanagh. It is possible that his father was James Irvine, a doctor in Enniskillen. Other sources give the father's name as John; it seems likely that the family was related to the gentry family of Irvines of Castle Irvine. His mother may have been Ann Armstrong ('Armstrong' appears in the names of two of his own children). There were at least three (possibly six) sons and two daughters in the family. Irvine attended school in Enniskillen and is said to have studied at Trinity College Dublin, though his name does not appear in the list of graduates. After a short time as a cornet of dragoons, he studied medicine (it is said, with the noted teacher George Cleghorn) and then went into the navy as a ship's surgeon. He saw service in the Seven Years' War (1756–63), but resigned and with two of his brothers settled (1764) in Carlisle, Pennsylvania, where he set up a medical practice.

Like many emigrants from Ulster, Irvine supported efforts to achieve American independence in the years after 1770, and in 1774 attended the Provincial Congress of Pennsylvania. In 1776 he was commissioned colonel in a Pennsylvania regiment, and (after recruiting soldiers and equipping the regiment himself) joined the American attack on Canada; the Americans were defeated at Trois Rivières, and he was captured. He was well treated, and was paroled on 3 August 1776; he was not free to re-engage in the war till he was formally exchanged (6 May 1778). He was made a brigadier-general in the Continental army (1779), and took part in unsuccessful attacks around New York (1780). As commander of Fort Pitt (now Pittsburgh) from 1781, he was charged with defence of the north-western frontier, and restored discipline after mutinies in the Pennsylvanian regiments. The fort was under-manned, and Irvine authorised volunteer sorties into the Native American-controlled upper Ohio valley; as a result, innocent natives, who were Moravian converts, were massacred (1782). American forces were later defeated and tortured in reprisal attacks by natives.

Irvine resigned his command in November 1783 when the war was over. He received a land grant, spent the rest of his life in public affairs in Pennsylvania, and was a member of the Confederation Congress in 1786–8. He recommended in 1785 the purchase of land to allow that state access to Lake Erie, and served on commissions to establish boundaries and to lay out several towns, including Erie, Pennsylvania. He was a delegate (1790) to the convention that established a new constitution for Pennsylvania, and during 1793–5 he served in the third US Congress.

Irvine was sent as a commissioner to try to defuse the controversy in western Pennsylvania, where the mainly Scotch-Irish settlers resented what they saw as government interference; the imposition of taxes on their whiskey distilling was particularly unpopular. Though he expressed sympathy for their difficult circumstances, in a letter to President Washington, he accepted command as major-general of the state militia when the discontent in the back country became the 'whiskey rebellion' of 1794. He was one of the founding members of the elite Society of the Cincinnati, and was its president from 1801. His influence on Pennsylvanian politics continued till his death in Philadelphia of cholera, 29 July 1804. He married (perhaps in 1772) Anne Callender in Carlisle, Pennsylvania. They had five sons and six daughters; three sons had military careers.

Linde Lunney

SOURCES
Who was who in America: historical volume 1607–1896 (1963); Mark M. Boatner,
Cassell's biographical dictionary of the American War of Independence 1763–1783
(1966); *Biographical directory of the American Congress 1774–1971* (1971); *Webster's
American military biographies* (1978); *ANB*; material from
http://www.irvineclan.com/wi1741.htm, and
http://www.irvineclan.com/irvine.htm; http://www.bradfordhouse.org/rebell.HTM
(accessed Apr. 2001)

Jackson, Elizabeth
c. 1740–81
American patriot and mother of President Andrew Jackson

Elizabeth Jackson was born in or near the town of Carrickfergus, Co.
Antrim. Her father's name was Hutchinson, but this is all we know for
certain of her parents. Some sources claim that his name was Francis Cyrus
Hobart Hutchinson. While there were several well-known eighteenth-
century Francis Hutchinsons/Hutchesons, multiple Christian names were
not usual at that period, and the middle names of Cyrus and Hobart are
virtually unattested in early eighteenth-century Ulster. In later life,
Elizabeth Jackson reportedly talked of her father's voluntary service against
an enemy force in Carrickfergus: it seems likely that this was the so-called
'invasion' of the town in 1760 by the French privateer François Thurot. A
contemporary source lists a Mr John Hutchinson as one of the valiant
defenders of the town, and this was possibly Elizabeth's father. Her mother
may have been a Lisle, but more likely a Leslie, and thus would have been
related to a Captain James Leslie, who took emigrants from Carrickfergus
to South Carolina in 1755.

Passengers on this ship almost certainly included Elizabeth's five older
sisters and their husbands (two of whom were Leslies, perhaps their
cousins) and their families. They settled in an area that was known as the
Waxhaws, in the backwoods of North and South Carolina. Left in Ireland,
Elizabeth Hutchinson married Andrew Jackson, apparently in 1759, in the
Anglican parish church in Carrickfergus, though the family later identified
as Presbyterian.

Though they may have suffered from rent increases and other financial
impositions, such as Anglican tithes, stories of the family's poverty in
Ireland before emigration clearly derive from the American mythology of
the poor backwoods boy becoming president. The Jacksons and
Hutchinsons were well connected in Ireland, possibly related to Anglican
clergy, and fairly well-to-do. (In 1781 a Carrickfergus relative left the young
Andrew Jackson a substantial legacy of over £300.) Elizabeth and her sisters

were all literate. Andrew and Elizabeth Jackson sold their property in Carrickfergus, possibly including an inn, and emigrated in 1765 with their two infant sons and with Elizabeth's only brother to join her sisters and scores of former Antrim neighbours settled in America.

Poverty and misfortune were waiting for them on the poor land in north-west South Carolina. Andrew Jackson, too late to secure a better property, took up 200 heavily wooded acres and struggled alone to clear the land and build a cabin. In February 1767, aged just twenty-nine, he died following an accident involving a heavy log. His widow, in the last month of pregnancy, had no other support and had to move in with one of her sisters. Three weeks later, on 15 March 1767, Andrew Jackson junior was born and faced a very uncertain future. Elizabeth Jackson's sister Jane Crawford and her husband James Crawford gave them a home. Elizabeth was involved in all the work in the house and farm, as her sister was an invalid, and she helped raise her nephews as well as her own boys.

When the stirrings of revolution came in the early 1770s, the family were ardent supporters of the patriot cause, all the more so after open warfare broke out in 1775. Elizabeth Jackson is said to have helped nurse wounded rebels after a skirmish in the Waxhaws in 1780. Her oldest son, Hugh, died of heat exhaustion fighting the British at Stono Ferry in coastal South Carolina in 1779, and the two younger sons, still in their early teens, immediately joined the rebel forces. They were taken prisoner in their aunt's house, which was then pillaged by the British. Both young Jacksons were wounded, and both also contracted smallpox in the prison camp at Camden, South Carolina. Elizabeth Jackson negotiated a prisoner exchange to secure the release of her sons, travelling forty miles with two horses to bring the boys back. Andrew was on foot, without coat or shoes, and badly malnourished. The older boy, Robert, died two days after the return to the Waxhaws. Elizabeth nursed Andrew for weeks, but, when he was recovering, she left him to travel 160 miles, through wartime conditions, to Charleston, South Carolina, to try to find her Crawford nephews.

After only a few days visiting and nursing prisoners on the prison ships in Charleston harbour, Elizabeth Jackson contracted fever and died in November 1781. Andrew learned of his mother's death when he received a small bundle of her possessions, perhaps including a small Bible she habitually carried. From the age of fourteen, he was on his own. He remembered her principles and precepts throughout his life (though not always living by them), and remained bitterly antagonistic to the British.

Andrew Jackson later tried to find where his mother was buried, so that her remains could be brought to rest in the graveyard of Waxhaw Presbyterian church beside his father and brothers, but her gravesite had been lost. Three later memorials in Charleston and Waxhaw, erected by the

Daughters of the American Revolution and others, preserve the memory of Elizabeth Jackson's contribution to American history.

The family's anti-British sentiment could have derived originally from Elizabeth Jackson's experiences in Ireland, or from maltreatment in America. Either way, it poses a clear ideological difficulty for twenty-first-century unionist Ulster-Scots who might seek to adopt President Andrew Jackson as 'one of their own'.

Linde Lunney

SOURCES
Belfast News Letter, 23 May 1755; 25 Aug. 1944; John Francis Durand, *Genuine and curious memoirs of the famous Captain Thurot* (1760), 32; Robert H. White, 'Elizabeth Hutchinson Jackson, the mother of President Andrew Jackson', *Tennessee Historical Magazine*, series 2, iii, no. 3 (Apr. 1935), 179–84; H. W. Brands, *Andrew Jackson: his life and times* (2005); Sheila Ingle, 'Elizabeth Hutchinson Jackson: the mother of President Andrew Jackson' (7 July 2014), sheilaingle.com; D. F. Lesslie, 'The genealogy of the Lesslie family since 1750', Rootsweb, listsearches.rootsweb.com/th/read/HUTCHINSON/2000-02/0951117102; internet material accessed Nov. 2017

Johnson, Guy
c. 1740–88
American loyalist

Guy Johnson was born in Ireland, possibly in Co. Meath, son of John Johnson, landowner, and Catherine Johnson (née Nangle). His uncle Sir William Johnson was an influential figure in colonial America, and Guy decided to seek his fortune there; he sailed on HMS *Prince* in 1755, serving as a midshipman. Arriving in the colonies, he fought in the Seven Years' War (1756–63), commanding a company of rangers. With Sir William superintendent of Indian affairs, Guy was appointed a secretary to the northern Indian department, and in 1762 was made Sir William's deputy agent. A talented draughtsman, he made important drawings of the region for the British authorities. In 1763 he married his cousin Mary ('Polly') Johnson, youngest daughter of Sir William. Continuing to serve in the army, he became a colonel and adjutant-general of the New York militia and was elected to the New York assembly (1773–5).

The death of his uncle (July 1774) came at a volatile time in colonial relations with Britain. Guy was appointed acting superintendent of Indian affairs, and worked to secure the loyalty of Native American tribes in the face of revolutionary disturbances. To clarify his jurisdiction, he went to England in November 1775 accompanied by his friend, the Mohawk leader known as Joseph Brant (1742–1807); he returned in summer 1776, having lost responsibility for the Canadian territory. Delegating authority for the Indian department to subordinates, he remained in New York, expecting the rebellion to be swiftly extinguished. From 1779 he directed Native American and loyalist raids against the rebels, destroying food supplies intended for the revolutionary army. His cousin and brother-in-law Sir John Johnson succeeded him in the Indian department in 1783, and Guy returned to London to press his claims for government compensation for lost property. His case dragged on, and he died, apparently in poverty, on 5 March 1788. His wife predeceased him, on 11 July 1775; they had four children, but only two daughters survived to adulthood.

Frederick West, the artist famed for the 'Death of Wolfe' (1770), made a portrait of Johnson, probably during his 1775–6 visit to England. 'Guy Johnson and David Hill' holds an important position in Native American iconography: neither Johnson nor Hill (a Mohawk chief) indicate a position of superiority; both are seen to represent allied nations. Johnson is shown in a mixture of British and native clothing, emphasising his knowledge of Native American customs, and his respect for the various traditions he sought to defend.

Patrick M. Geoghegan

SOURCES
Webb; *DNB*; Eileen MacCarrill, 'Johnsons—lineal descendants of Uí Néill', *North Munster Antiquarian Journal*, xvii (1975), 60–61; M. W. Hamilton, *Sir William Johnson: colonial American* (1976); *DAB*; *DCB*; Carl Waldman, *Who was who in Native American history* (1990); Leslie Reinhardt, 'British and Indian identities in a picture by Benjamin West', *Eighteenth-Century Studies*, xxxi (1998), 283–305; *ANB*

Johnson, Sir William
1715–74
Superintendent of Indian affairs in colonial America

Sir William Johnson was born at Smithtown, Co. Meath, one of seven children (three sons and four daughters) of Christopher Johnson, tenant farmer, and Anne Johnson (née Warren). The Johnsons claimed to be a 'line honorable in its alliances': both the Johnsons and Warrens conformed to the Church of Ireland, probably during the early eighteenth century.

In early 1738 Johnson arrived in America to oversee the Mohawk valley estate of his uncle, Vice-admiral Sir Peter Warren, at Warrensburg, New York, near the mouth of the Schoharie river and covering twenty-two square miles (57 sq. km). By 1740 he had built his own home, Mount

Johnson, across the river from Warrensburg. To run the household he chose a German indentured servant, Catherine Weisenberg, who became the mother of three of his children: a son, Sir John Johnson (who became a loyalist leader in the American revolution, later settling in Canada), and two daughters, Ann ('Nancy') and Mary. For the farm he recruited twelve families in Co. Meath and also brought along as a companion his cousin, Michael Tyrrell, who later grew tired of frontier life and gained a naval commission through Peter Warren's aid. This began a pattern (which Johnson followed throughout his career) of settling Irish immigrants on his estates, as well as Palatine Germans: these served as a buffer against the often antagonistic Albany Dutch, who had long held a virtual monopoly on trade with the Iroquois and also carried on an illegal trade with the French and Native Americans in Canada.

During this period, Johnson began trading with the Six Nations (Iroquois confederacy), as well as supplying the settlers in the Mohawk valley. His close relationship with the Six Nations, particularly the Mohawks, led him into the political and military arenas, influencing his ideas of how the colonies should manage questions of trade and westward expansion. By 1745–8, when he participated in the war of the Austrian succession (called 'King George's war' in North America), he had already gained the confidence of Tiyanoga, a Mohawk sachem (administrative chief), known to the Dutch as 'King Hendrick', who had travelled to England in 1709–10 and again in 1740. Johnson's friendship with the Mohawks was so great that he was adopted into the tribe and renamed Warraghiyagey ('Chief Big Business' or 'Doer of great things'). Johnson learned the Mohawk language, and he also adopted their clothing and customs when among them.

In 1746 the New York assembly voted to provide Johnson with funds to supply Fort Oswego on Lake Ontario and he was named 'colonel of the … Six Nations and commissary for Indian affairs' by the royal governor of New York, George Clinton (son of the Irishman Charles Clinton). Returning to the Mohawk valley following the end of the war, in 1748 Johnson began building Fort Johnson, a stone house still in existence. Johnson participated in the Albany Congress (1754) which helped formulate British policy toward native peoples. In April 1755 the crown confirmed Johnson as superintendent of Indian affairs with full powers to treat with the Six Nations and their allies, and he was also commissioned major-general by the northern colonial governments.

Increasing French encroachments on the north-western frontier eventually led to the Seven Years' War (officially 1756–63, though it began and ended earlier in North America, where it is called the 'French and Indian War'). Although Johnson's expedition to capture the French fort at Crown Point failed, he soundly defeated the French under Baron Dieskau at Lake George (September 1755) and later established Forts Edward and

William Henry. In November 1755 the king made him a baronet (only the second in the American colonies). He participated in the siege of Niagara (1759), which fell to him on 25 July, and in 1760 he served with Gen. Jeffery Amherst in the capture of Montreal. That year the Mohawks bestowed the title of sachem on him. In 1761 he journeyed to Detroit, part of a diplomatic mission to pacify the Native Americans of that region. In 1762 he founded Johnstown, New York, where he established his principal residence.

After Catherine Weisenberg's death (1759), Mary ('Molly') Brant, daughter of the sachem Nichuls Brant (Aroghyiadecker) and sister of Joseph Brant, the Mohawk leader during the American revolution, came to manage the household, first at Fort Johnson and later at the Georgian-style Johnson Hall, built in 1763, still in existence. Between 1759 and 1773 she bore William nine children, of whom eight survived, two sons and six daughters. One son, Peter Johnson, was killed aged seventeen fighting on the British side during the American revolution, and Molly (known also as Degonwadonti) herself led Mohawk warriors. After that war, Molly and her family settled in Kingston, Ontario, where she died in 1796, about sixty years old. Sir William Johnson had died on 11 July 1774, aged fifty-nine, probably from cirrhosis of the liver, undoubtedly a result of years of hard drinking and entertaining Indians and Europeans at Fort Johnson and Johnson Hall, which were renowned centres of hospitality in the Mohawk valley.

Portraits of Johnson may be found in the Public Archives of Canada, Albany Institute of History and Art, New York Historical Society, and Derby Museum and Art Gallery (the last, by Benjamin West, showing him rescuing a French officer from a tomahawk-wielding Iroquois). His papers were edited by the New York State Division of Archives, Albany (13 vols, 1921–62).

James E. Doan

SOURCES
Arthur Pound, in collaboration with Richard E. Day, *Johnson of the Mohawks: a biography of Sir William Johnson, Irish immigrant, Mohawk war chief, American soldier, empire builder* (1930, repr. 1971); James T. Flexner, *Lord of the Mohawks: a biography of Sir William Johnson* (1959, rev. ed. 1979); Milton W. Hamilton, *Sir William Johnson: colonial American, 1715–1763* (1976); Paul Redmond Drew, 'Sir William Johnson – Indian superintendent', *Early America Review*, i, no. 2 (fall 1996) [electronic journal]

Johnston, John
1762–1828
Fur trader

John Johnston was born on 25 August 1762 near Portrush, Co. Antrim, son of William Johnston and Elizabeth Johnston (née McNeil). The family, which had come from Scotland two generations earlier, owned Craige, an estate near the Giant's Causeway. Johnston's father served in the Royal Navy during the Seven Years' War (1756–63) and afterwards was appointed surveyor in Portrush and the barony of Dunluce. He also designed and built the waterworks for Belfast, but died about 1769, when Johnston was seven, leaving the family in difficult circumstances. Although he did not have a conventional education, Johnston developed a fondness for books and literature. At age seventeen he went to Belfast to manage the waterworks. However, the lease for the waterworks was not renewed and in 1789 he made plans to seek his fortune in British North America, sailing for Quebec in June 1790 with letters of introduction to the governor, Gen. Lord Dorchester (Guy Carleton), from Lord Hawkesbury, president of the Board of Trade, and several others.

Dorchester was unable to offer Johnston an appointment, but in Montreal Johnston met a friend from Ireland, Andrew Todd, nephew of Isaac Todd (b. *c.* 1742, in Ireland), of the fur traders Todd, McGill & Company, who gave him a position. Johnston spent the winter learning French outside Montreal, and in May 1791 joined Todd travelling to Michilimackinac, on Mackinaw Island, Michigan. Learning the trade during the summer, Johnston was sent with several French-Canadians to winter at the Native American settlement of La Pointe, on the south shore of Lake Superior. Abandoned by his assistants, Johnston survived the winter, traded furs, and helped the elderly father of the chief of the La Pointe Ojibway band, Wabojeeg (White Fisher). He also fell in love with Oshaguscodawaqua (whom he later called Susan), Wabojeeg's young daughter. Because Europeans tended to abandon their Native American wives, Johnston was told that in order to marry her he must wait a year and then promise not to leave her. He sold his furs in Montreal and returned the following spring to marry her, first at La Pointe and then in a Christian ceremony at Fort St Joseph. The marriage was a happy one, also giving Johnston excellent access to the native people in the region; but returning to Ireland became difficult.

Johnston dominated the trade in furs along the south shore of Lake Superior for many years. In 1793 he moved to Sault Sainte Marie, sometimes operating as an independent, sometimes working for the North West Company or the American Fur Company. At the Sault he built a fine house, well furnished with books. He visited Ireland in 1809 to inspect

Craige, the estate he had inherited from his mother in 1803. He arrived in Cork with his nine-year-old daughter Obah-dahm-wawn-gezzhago-quay (Woman of the Green Prairie), or Jane, whom he left with a great-aunt in Wexford while he made his way to Dublin and Co. Antrim. He also travelled to London, perhaps hoping for appointments for his sons, and was asked by Lord Selkirk to lead a planned settlement at Red River in western Canada. Despite the urging of his family that he should remain in Ireland, Johnston and his daughter sailed from Liverpool in June 1810.

Johnston's thoughts of possibly settling in Montreal were interrupted by the War of 1812. While he was assisting British forces in the defence of Mackinaw Island, American troops burned his property at Sault Sainte Marie. Nevertheless, he rebuilt his fur business, working largely for the American Fur Company. In 1819–20 Johnston returned to Ireland and England to sell his estate in Co. Antrim and to seek damages in London for his losses during the war. During his absence, Mrs Johnston intervened in a dispute between the local Native Americans and the governor of the Michigan Territory, enabling the United States to acquire land on which Fort Brady was built. By the 1820s Johnston's house was again a centre of culture and hospitality on the frontier. Johnston died on 22 September 1828.

John and Susan Johnston had eight children: Lewis Saurin served the British Indian Department; George became a fur trader and Indian agent for the United States Bureau of Indian Affairs; William served as an interpreter for the US government; John McDougal worked as an interpreter first for Henry Rowe Schoolcraft and then the US government; Jane married Henry Rowe Schoolcraft, explorer, ethnologist, and Indian agent at Sault Sainte Marie; Eliza did not marry; Charlotte married the Rev. William McMurray, an Anglican missionary at the Sault; and Anne Maria married James L. Schoolcraft. Material relating to John Johnston can be found in the George Johnston papers, Bayliss Public Library, Sault Sainte Marie, Michigan; George Johnston papers, Burton Historical Collection, Detroit Public Library; and Henry Rowe Schoolcraft papers, Library of Congress.

Francis M. Carroll

SOURCES

DCB; Henry Rowe Schoolcraft, *Personal memoirs of a residence of thirty years with the Indian tribes of the American frontiers, with brief notices of passing events, facts and opinions, A.D. 1812 to A.D. 1842* (1851); John Johnston, 'An account of Lake Superior, 1792–1807', L. R. Masson (ed.), *Les bourgeois de la Compagnie du Nord-Ouest* (1890); C. H. Chapman, 'The historic Johnston family of the "Soo"', *Michigan Pioneer and Historical Society Historical Collections*, xxxii (1903), 305–53; Henry Rowe Schoolcraft, 'Memoir of John Johnston', *Michigan Pioneer and Historical Society Collections*, xxxvi (1908), 53–90

Kirkpatrick, James
c. 1692–1770
Physician and poet

James Kirkpatrick (Kilpatrick, Killpatrick) was born at Carrickfergus, Co. Antrim, into a commercial family. He matriculated (1708) at Edinburgh University but left before graduating and returned to Ireland, where he became a medical practitioner. He had little success, and in search of fortune emigrated to South Carolina (1717) to join his uncle, David Killpatrick (d. *c.* 1724), and established a practice in Charleston among the merchant and official classes. Subsequently appointed attending physician to St Philip's Hospital, where he ministered to the poor, in the early 1730s he established a pharmacy which was the principal source of medicines in the town. He married (1727) Elizabeth Hepworth, daughter of the secretary of the colony, and in 1733 was joint recipient of a royal grant of 230 acres.

On the outbreak of a virulent smallpox epidemic (1738), he was one of the first to engage in the controversial practice of inoculation. Persuaded first by Mr Mowbray, surgeon of a British man-of-war in Charleston harbour, he became its most energetic practitioner, spurred perhaps by the death of his two-year-old son from smallpox. Although many doctors at this time would not have exposed their own families to the risks of inoculation, he inoculated his eldest son and his daughter, a younger son having previously recovered from the illness. He defended inoculation in the *South Carolina Gazette* and became involved in a much publicised pamphlet war with Thomas Dale (1700–50), a prominent and respected figure in Charleston, about the correct methods of inoculation, and wrote *A full and clear reply to Doct. T. Dale, wherein the real impropriety of blistering with cantharides in the first fever of the smallpox is plainly demonstrated* (Charleston, 1739). Killpatrick's superior technique lay in his application of an attenuated virus to healthy persons. Inoculation was subsequently prohibited by the Carolina assembly, which perhaps influenced his decision to leave Charleston. He served as a ship's surgeon on the 1739 expedition led by James Edward Oglethorpe (1696–1785) against the Spanish at St Augustine, Florida, before settling in London (1742), where he changed his name to Kirkpatrick (possibly to distance himself from the Charleston controversy) and qualified as a doctor.

He publicised the success of inoculation in his *Essay on inoculation occasioned by the small-pox being brought into South Carolina in the year 1738* (London, revised ed. 1743; previously published in Charleston, 1738); of the 800 inoculations he had performed, only eight patients died. It rapidly became a standard work. On the outbreak of the smallpox epidemic in London in 1746, which witnessed the highest mortality since 1629, Kirkpatrick assisted Isaac Maddox (1697–1759), bishop of

Worcester, in the founding of the pioneering Middlesex County Hospital for the Smallpox (1746), known by 1752 as the Small-Pox and Inoculation Hospital, where treatment was given free of charge to the working classes. Maddox advised and sponsored Kirkpatrick's authorship of *The analysis of inoculation comprising the history, theory and practice of it* (1754; 3rd ed. 1761); translated into Dutch, German, and French, it brought him international fame and recognition, became the leading monograph on the subject, and has been used by all subsequent historians.

He became the leading inoculator and made an important contribution towards the widespread acceptance of inoculation in England, though his claim to its revival, which was accepted by contemporaries and subsequent historians, has been latterly attributed to self-advertisement. He inoculated members of the British and French aristocracy and his writings and reputation were influential in the acceptance of inoculation in France during the 1750s when smallpox epidemics swept through Europe.

As a poet, he celebrated the British empire of the seas and while living in South Carolina wrote *The sea-piece; a narrative, philosophical and descriptive poem. In five cantos* (composed 1717–38; revised ed. London, 1750), which has been described as 'the most ... ambitious meditation on Britain's maritime destiny composed by any eighteenth-century poet' (Shields, 25–6). An admirer of Alexander Pope (1688–1744), he saluted him as the poetic lord of the empire and wrote several poems including his anonymous *An epistle to Alex. Pope Esq. from South Carolina* (1737) in response to attacks made on Pope after the publication of his *Dunciad variorum* (1729), and translated some of Pope's elegies into Latin as *Elegia Popi in memoriam* ... (1744). In his later years he translated several of the works of S. A. D. Tissot (1728–97), including *Advice to the people in general in regard to their health* (1765; 6th ed. 1793) and an annotated version of *An essay on the disorders of people of fashion; and a treatise on the diseases incident to literary persons* (1772). He died in London in 1770. A bibliography of his writings was published by H. R. Viets, 'Boston Medical Library' (*New England Journal of Medicine*, ccxlvii (18 Sept. 1952), 433).

Helen Andrews

SOURCES

James Kilpatrick, *An essay on inoculation occasioned by the small-pox being brought into South Carolina in the year 1738* (1743); J. I. Waring, 'James Killpatrick and smallpox inoculation in Charlestown', *Annals of Medical History*, x (1938), 301–08; Genevieve Miller, *The adoption of inoculation for smallpox in England and France* (1957); J. R. Smith, *The speckled monster: smallpox in England, 1670–1970* (1987); D. S. Shields, *Oracles of empire: poetry, politics, and commerce in British America 1690–1750* (1990); Peter Razzell, *The conquest of smallpox: the impact of inoculation on smallpox mortality in eighteenth-century Britain* (1977); *ANB*

Knox, William
1732–1810
Government official and polemicist

William Knox was born at Clones, Co. Monaghan, son of Thomas Knox, physician, and Nicola Knox (née King). His father was a devout Protestant, with strong Calvinist tendencies (he claimed descent from John Knox), and these religious principles became a rigid part of William's character from an early age. Educated locally, he may have entered Trinity College Dublin, but was soon involved in politics as a supporter of Sir Richard Cox (1702–66) during the political controversies of 1753–6. Deciding to seek his fortune abroad, in 1756 he was appointed provost marshal of the American colony of Georgia. There he established a large plantation worked by slaves, and served on the provincial council. Returning to London in 1762, he became an unofficial adviser to British ministers on imperial affairs. In 1765 he was dismissed as a colonial agent for Georgia because of his pamphlet *The claim of the colonies*, which defended the right of the British parliament to pass the controversial Stamp Act (1765), even though he questioned its efficacy.

Aligning himself with George Grenville (1712–70), who as prime minister (1763–5) had devised the Stamp Act, Knox became a leading pamphleteer and political adviser. His *Present state of the nation* (1768) is famous for outlining the theory of an imperial framework where both colony and home country worked in harmony for the greater good of the empire. As the work attacked the Rockingham whigs, it was answered by their chief polemicist, Edmund Burke, in his *Observations on a late state of the nation* (1769).

Knox's permanent search for financial security saw him accept office, and in 1770 he became under-secretary for the new American department. His pamphlets in defence of Lord North's administration widened the breach with the colonies, however. Always interested in Irish affairs, he pushed successfully for trade concessions (1778–80), even though he considered Ireland a colony. With the American War of Independence he lost his Georgia plantation, and after the fall of the North ministry in 1782 was dismissed from office by a vengeful Rockingham government. Becoming a political adviser for hire, he was much in demand for his expertise on Anglo-American affairs. He frequently defended slavery on evangelical grounds, and argued that it allowed for the education and conversion of Africa. In 1790 he received compensation for the loss of his properties and decided to retire. He became a landowner and farmer in England and Wales, but the lure of politics was too great and he became an agent for the provinces of New Brunswick and Prince Edward Island as well as engaging in various public controversies. He urged a union between Britain and

Ireland in the 1790s, but this was as much to threaten the Irish Protestants into granting Catholic rights as anything else. He died on 25 August 1810 at Great Ealing, Middlesex.

He married (1756) Letitia Ford, from Ireland, who had a large fortune; they had seven children. His son Thomas was colonel in a volunteer regiment that Knox had founded in 1793, but was later dismissed.

Knox is widely regarded as one of the most influential imperialist thinkers of the eighteenth century. A brilliant but egotistical man, whose political thinking was largely paternalistic, he helped develop, and later defended, the system of policies that led to the American revolution.

Patrick M. Geoghegan

SOURCES
Webb; *DNB*; *Irish Book Lover*, ii (1910), 25; E. H. Stuart Jones, *The last invasion of Britain* (1950); Richard Koebner, *Empire* (1961); Leland J. Bellot, 'Evangelicals and the defense of slavery in Britain's old colonial empire', *Journal of Southern History*, xxxvii (1971), 19–40; Leland J. Bellot, *William Knox: the life and thought of an eighteenth-century imperialist* (1977); *ANB*

Lewis, Andrew
1720–81
Soldier and colonist

Andrew Lewis was born on 9 October 1720 in Co. Donegal, son of John Lewis, farmer, and Margaret Lewis (née Lynn). His father, of Huguenot descent, emigrated with his family to America after being involved in an agrarian dispute. According to Appleton, his father had actually killed his landlord after an illegal attempt to evict the family. They lived for a time in Pennsylvania and then moved *c.* 1732 to Augusta County, Virginia, where they were among the first white settlers.

Andrew Lewis initially worked as a land agent and surveyor, buying large tracts of land for himself along the Virginian frontier. He held a senior rank in the Virginia militia and, on the outbreak of the Seven Years' War (1756–63), took part in an unsuccessful expedition commanded by George Washington against the French forts on the upper Ohio. Promoted to major, he was highly regarded by Washington and was present at the capture of Fort Necessity. In 1756 he commanded the Sandy Creek expedition, but during the course of this arduous trek his army ran out of food and most of his soldiers deserted. Captured during Maj. James Grant's expedition to Fort Duquesne (1758), he remained a prisoner of war at Montreal till the end of the war.

Returning to Virginia, he continued to acquire land, and by the 1760s owned properties in the Greenbrier valley and also over 1,400 acres near Staunton. In 1768 he served as a commissioner for Virginia, concluding a treaty with the Six Nations at Fort Stanwix in New York state. He also served as the sheriff of Augusta and Botetourt counties and sometimes acted as the county magistrate. During the Indian war of 1774, he defeated a large force of Shawnee, led by Chief Cornstalk, at Point Pleasant. The Shawnee later concluded a treaty in which they ceded all their territory south of the Ohio. A member of the Virginia house of burgesses, Lewis attended the conventions of May and June 1775. In March 1776 he was appointed brigadier-general in the Continental army and was prominent in the campaign to drive Governor Dunmore's loyalist forces from the Chesapeake Bay area. He had expected, however, to be given the rank of major-general, and when this was not forthcoming he resigned in protest in April 1777. In 1780 he was appointed a member of the Virginia executive council. He contracted a fever while travelling to his home on the upper Roanoke river and died on 26 September 1781 in Bedford county, Virginia.

Andrew Lewis was, by all accounts, an impressive if somewhat difficult character. He typified the early settlers in Virginia, and his attitude to the local Native American population was on some occasions conciliatory, and on others highly aggressive. A strict disciplinarian, he was often at odds with the men under his command. He married Elizabeth Givens; they had seven children. A statue of him was later placed on one of the pedestals of the Washington monument in Richmond, Virginia.

His brothers were also prominent members in the Virginia administration. Thomas Lewis (1718–90) was a member of the Virginia house of burgesses, while his younger brother, William Lewis (1724–1811) was a soldier and served under Andrew's command. Yet another brother, Charles Lewis (d. 10 October 1774), was killed at the battle of Point Pleasant.

David Murphy

SOURCES
Appletons; Webb; J. S. Crone, *A concise dictionary of Irish biography* (1928); *DAB*; *ANB*; Patricia Givens Johnson, *General Andrew Lewis of Roanoke and Greenbrier* (1980)

Logan, James
1674–1751
Scientist and public servant

James Logan was born on 20 October 1674 at Lurgan, Co. Armagh, son of Patrick Logan, a schoolmaster, originally a Church of Scotland clergyman who had become a Quaker, and his wife, Isabel Logan (née Hume), who had both left Scotland to avoid persecution. Educated initially by his father, James was largely self-taught and read voraciously throughout his life. In 1690 his family moved to Bristol, and in 1694 he was put in charge of the Friar Meeting-House Quaker school there, replacing his father who had returned to Ireland. Around 1697–9 he attempted to work in the linen trade, before deciding to accompany the Quaker leader, William Penn, to America. James Logan's brother William (1686–1757) remained in Bristol where he became a physician; he corresponded regularly with James on scientific matters.

In 1711 Logan became engaged in the fur trade, using methods that were certainly unscrupulous and bordered on the illegal: he sold rum to the Native Americans and left many fur traders in debt. As Penn's secretary, he was closely involved in many of the details of the settlement of Pennsylvania. He was a respected figure in his own right, serving as secretary of the province and clerk of the provincial council of Pennsylvania (1701–17). Other prominent offices followed: he served as mayor of Philadelphia (1722–3), was a chief justice in the supreme court of Pennsylvania (1731–9), and was acting governor of Pennsylvania (1736–7). Throughout his life he continued to represent the interests of Penn and Penn's heirs as administrator, lawyer, and merchant.

Through his investments in land, and his trade with the Native Americans, with whom he was always on good terms despite his practices, Logan quickly became very wealthy. A well-read man, he had an extensive library, and was recognised for his expertise in mathematics, natural history, and astronomy. He published works on optics, and botany, and advised Benjamin Franklin on his researches. In particular, his pioneering work on the pollination of plants, begun in 1727, marked a breakthrough in plant hybridisation, as he recognised that maize reproduced sexually.

On 9 December 1714 he married Sarah Read, the daughter of Charles Read, a merchant; they had five children. He died on 31 October 1751, at Germantown, Pennsylvania. Aristocratic in bearing, and in outlook, Logan is recognised as a leading intellectual scientist of his time. His most important scientific contribution, however, was not his own research but his role as advisor to others. In 1742 he decided to bequeath his vast library to the public, and this request was carried out by his son, James, after his death. At first housed at the Bibliotheca Loganiana, the 2,184 volumes are now stored at the Library Company of Philadelphia, and are recognised as the finest collection assembled in pre-independence America. Logan's eldest son, William (1718–76), succeeded him as the Penn family advisor.

Patrick M. Geoghegan

SOURCES
DNB; *DAB*; F. B. Tolles, *James Logan and the culture of provincial America* (1957); Edwin Wolf II, *The library of James Logan of Philadelphia* (1974); Clark A. Elliott, *Biographical dictionary of American science* (1979); Arthur Raistrick, *Quakers in science and industry* (1993)

Lyon, Matthew
1750–1822
Politician

Matthew Lyon was born on 14 July 1750 in Co. Wicklow, son of a farmer who died when Matthew was a child. Educated in Dublin, Matthew Lyon emigrated to America in 1765, paying for his passage with three years' indentured service. In 1774 he moved to Vermont where he purchased property. He joined a local regiment and served as a lieutenant in various campaigns on the Canadian border, where he was censured for the indiscipline of his troops. He resigned or possibly (as his enemies later claimed) was discharged from the army and joined the Vermont militia. He established various entrepreneurial interests in Vermont – an ironworks, a printing-press, and other ventures – and became a leading figure in the community.

When Vermont joined the new United States in 1791, Lyon ran unsuccessfully for the house and senate. Finally elected to the House of Representatives (1796), he cut an isolated figure, both because of his republican views and his unique manner. He was lampooned as an ignorant backwoodsman, but this was for the most part an unfair caricature, and he possessed many good ideas about the new nation. A major controversy arose after 30 January 1798 when he spat in the face of Roger Griswold, a member of the house who had disparaged his military record. Two weeks later, in a dramatic confrontation, Griswold assaulted him with a cane on the floor of the house. The incident was satirised soon after in two poems: John Woodworth's *The spunkiad, or, Heroism improved* and John Carey's *The house of wisdom in a bustle.* Later in the year Lyon was found guilty on a largely spurious charge of libelling President Adams, fined $1,000, and sentenced to four months' imprisonment. This persecution only increased his popularity in Vermont, and he was re-elected in 1798 with a massive majority. In the 1800 election for president of the United States, he cast the decisive vote in favour of Thomas Jefferson, and became a Democratic hero in the process.

In 1801 he decided to move west, and settled in Eddyville, Kentucky, where he established more business interests. He remained active in politics, and represented the state in Congress (1802–10). In this period he established himself as a major debater, forcing a readjustment of previous opinions of him. Defeated in the 1810 election because of his opposition to the approaching war with Britain, he embarked on unwise speculations in building gunboats, which left him in financial penury. President Monroe, out of friendship, gave him in 1820 a federal office as representative to the Cherokee nation in Arkansas. He was again elected to the House of Representatives for Arkansas in the second territorial election (1822), but died the same year before he could take his seat.

In 1771 Lyon married a Miss Hosford, a niece of Ethan Allen. She died 1782, and the following year he married a widow, Beulah Galusha, a daughter of Governor Thomas Chittenden; he had three surviving children from the first union, and eight from the second. Lyon died on 1 August 1822, at Spadra Bluff, Arkansas. His son, Chittenden Lyon (1787–1842), followed him into politics, and held office for many years in Kentucky and in Congress. Matthew Lyon's move to Kentucky was the subject of a novel published in 1955 by Elizabeth A. Roe entitled *Aunt Leanna, or, Early scenes in Kentucky*.

Patrick M. Geoghegan

SOURCES

Pliny H. White, *The life and services of Matthew Lyon* (1858); Webb; J. Fairfax McLoughlin, *Matthew Lyon: the Hampden of Congress* (1900); R. J. Purcell, 'An Irish crusader for American democracy: Matthew Lyon', *Studies: an Irish Quarterly Review*, 25 (1936), 47–64; G. L. Montagno, 'Matthew Lyon, radical Jeffersonian, 1796–1801: a case study in partisan politics' (Ph.D. thesis, University of California, Berkeley, 1954); *DAB*

McGregor, James
1677?–1729
Presbyterian minister and emigrants' leader

James McGregor was born in Magilligan, Co. Londonderry, one of two known sons of Capt. McGregor, who also had at least one daughter. During the Williamite war (1688–91) the family took refuge in Derry city, and James is said to have fired the gun announcing the approach of the relieving ships. He was well educated, and probably graduated from Glasgow University. He preached for a time in Macosquin, but declined a call from that congregation and was ordained as minister in Aghadowey on 25 August 1701. McGregor was a fluent Irish-speaker, and one of the ministers authorised by the synod of 1710 to travel among the native Irish for at least three months each year to preach in Irish. Though the ambitious plan seems not to have been carried out, McGregor is known to have preached before Irish-speaking congregations in several counties, and in 1716 he was instructed by the presbytery to preach a sermon in Irish to a society of ministers who were to meet regularly to improve their command of the language. In May 1704 a scandalous 'flying report' alleged that the minister had been drunk in Coleraine; a special presbytery met, and accepted McGregor's statement that he had not been drunk, but had had several cans of ale, and that 'less might have serv'd'. He was exhorted to greater circumspection. In October 1706 he married Marion or Mary Ann Cargill, daughter of Aghadowey's elder David Cargill; her sister was married to a prominent merchant in Ballymoney, James McKeen, who was later a leader with McGregor of the emigration from the Bann valley to New Hampshire. Some sources state that McGregor's wife died in 1714, having had two children, and that he later married a daughter of James McKeen.

Economic conditions, as well as a perception among Presbyterians that their religious freedom was under threat in Ireland, led to a decision to seek opportunities in America. In March 1718 over 300 Presbyterians signed a petition to the colonial government. This was taken to America by the Rev. William Boyd; but, without waiting for a response, McGregor and McKeen, with others, organised the emigration of several hundred people from the Bann valley in several small ships, which sailed from Coleraine and Belfast. They reached the port of Boston in August 1718; Boyd had arrived in late July, but had not managed to secure any land for the settlers. McGregor and an Archibald Boyd presented, on 31 October 1718, a petition to the Massachusetts house of representatives, but though land was granted it was not surveyed until the following spring. Some of the settlers remained on the ship they had chartered, and spent a wretched winter frozen in sea ice at Casco Bay; McGregor was recommended by Cotton Mather, Boston's most influential clergyman, to the people of Dracut as their minister and teacher, and he passed the winter with them. In the spring of 1719 the scattered Ulster emigrants regrouped, and selected a tract of land near Haverhill; McGregor, whose commanding presence is frequently noted, preached from beneath an oak tree. McGergor's sermon, on a bleak text from the prophet Isaiah, has been described by local historians as thanksgiving for the establishment of a settlement first called Nutfield, and later known as Londonderry, New Hampshire, but seems rather to have been a cry of despair at the situation in which he and his hearers found themselves.

McGregor became their minister, the first Presbyterian minister in New England, and was prominent in local affairs; he carried a loaded gun always, even into the pulpit, for fear of attack by Native Americans, though it is said that his friendship with Philippe, marquis de Vaudreuil, governor of Canada, ensured that the community received some protection from natives. A meeting-house was built in 1722.

McGregor died of fever in New Hampshire on 5 March 1729; seven of his ten children survived him, along with his widow, who married his successor in the congregation, Matthew Clerk from Kilrea. McGregor's son David, the eldest son to survive to adulthood, became a Presbyterian minister in New Hampshire, and was more renowned there even than his father.

Linde Lunney

SOURCES
Charles Knowles Bolton, *Scotch Irish pioneers in Ulster and America* (1910; repr. 1967), *passim*; R. J. Dickson, *Ulster emigration to colonial America 1718–1775* (1966), 21, 26–8; T. H. Mullin, *Aghadowey: a parish and its linen industry* (1972), 40, 45–8; Roger Blaney, *Presbyterians and the Irish language* (1996), 24–6, 34–5; www.familysearch.com/search/af/individual_record.asp?recid+34656223; James E. Doan, 'The Eaglewing expedition (1636) and the settlement of Londonderry, New Hampshire (1719)', *Journal of Scotch-Irish Studies*, i, no. 1 (2000), 1–17; information from Helen Beall, family historian

McHenry, James
1753–1816
Doctor, soldier and statesman

James McHenry was born on 16 November 1753 in Ballymena, Co. Antrim, son of Daniel McHenry, merchant, and his wife, Agnes. Educated in Dublin, in 1771 he emigrated to America, where his family joined him in Philadelphia the following year. He attended the Newark Academy, Delaware; his predilection for poetry soon gave way to an interest in medicine, and he trained as a doctor in Philadelphia. When conflict between Britain and the colonies appeared inevitable in 1775, he volunteered for military service because of his dislike for England. With the outbreak of the War of Independence he served as a surgeon, and was briefly captured by the British, although he was later paroled and exchanged. On 15 May 1778 he was appointed secretary to Gen. George Washington, thus ending his medical career. Establishing a lifelong friendship with Washington, he was transferred (1780) to the staff of the French general, Lafayette. In 1781 he became a major, and was elected to the Maryland senate (1781–6). Appointed to Congress (1783–6), he was a Maryland delegate to the National Convention that drafted the constitution (1787). Although a committed federalist, he was not a clever theorist, and his greatest contribution was keeping a record of the proceedings. Through his many contacts, McHenry had a vast array of patronage at his disposal, which he dispensed liberally in Maryland between 1780 and 1795.

With Washington as first president of the USA, in January 1796 McHenry was appointed secretary of war, after three others had declined the office. He engaged in a sweeping restructuring of the army; Fort Whetstone in Baltimore was renamed 'Fort McHenry' in his honour. His role in the creation of the 'new army' was important, but he had little ability as a politician or an administrator, and Washington soon regretted his appointment. Although he continued to serve under the second president, John Adams, their relationship was tense and he was forced to resign in 1800. It seems he had often acted behind Adams's back, but the real problem appears to have been his easy-going manner; he was so affable he always deferred to whoever he was with at the time. Retiring to his estate at Fayetteville, near Baltimore, he opposed the War of 1812. When Fort McHenry was attacked by British rockets during this conflict, it inspired the writing of 'The star-spangled banner', the American national anthem. McHenry was president of the first Bible society, in Baltimore (1813). An invalid after 1814, he died on 3 May 1816. He married (8 January 1784) Margaret Allison Caldwell; they had four children, of whom a son and a daughter survived him.

Patrick M. Geoghegan

SOURCES
DAB; Richard H. Kohn, *Eagle and sword: the federalists and the creation of the military establishment in America* (1975); Noemie Emery, *Washington: a biography* (1976); J. B. Lyons, *Brief lives of Irish doctors 1600–1965* (1978); *ANB*

MacSparran, James
1693–1757
Clergyman

James MacSparran (McSparran) was born on 10 September 1693, probably in Dungiven, Co. Londonderry. He was the nephew of Archibald MacSparran, a Presbyterian minister and large landowner who had emigrated from the west of Scotland during persecutions there in the 1670s and 1680s. After being educated in Derry city, James attended the

University of Glasgow and was awarded an MA (5 March 1709). Back in Ulster, he was subsequently licensed as a Presbyterian minister under the guidance of his uncle Archibald. While little is known of his early life, he appears to have spoken Irish and to have preached in the language. After a number of years, having been accused of immorality, he left for America, becoming the pastor of the Congregational church of Bristol (December 1718), then in Massachusetts, now Rhode Island. He was almost immediately challenged on his ministerial credentials, as well as on grounds of fraud and immorality. Following an investigation, MacSparran was exonerated, but the Bristol church council suggested he confirm his credentials. He returned to England, where he was ordained first a deacon and then a priest in the Church of England (August–September 1720). He returned shortly afterwards to America (April 1721) as a missionary of the Society for the Propagation of the Gospel in Foreign Parts (SPG).

MacSparran was soon rector of St Paul's in Narragansett County, Rhode Island, holding services in Bristol, Freetown, Swansea, and Little Compton, attracting large numbers. He later founded the episcopal church in New London, Connecticut. He also owned both black and Amerindian slaves, though, unlike many of his contemporaries, he did not exclude them from his mission. Bishop George Berkeley visited in 1729, was escorted to view nearby tribes, and issued a report for the SPG on their conditions. While Oxford later conferred on MacSparran an honorary doctorate in sacred theology (1737), the 'Apostle of Narragansett' was held in less esteem by Quakers and independent sects. He was involved in a spurious, twenty-eight-year, legal dispute with the Dissenter Joseph Torrey over the Pettaquamscutt purchase before losing his claim in 1752. In the same period, his *Sacred dignity of the Christian priesthood vindicated* (1752) was critical of the irregularities of nonconforming ministers and provoked outrage among them. He expressed similar views in *America dissected* (1753, reprinted in the appendix of Wilkins Updike, *History of the episcopal Church of Narragansett* (1847)). That work also showed his deep, lifelong dislike of America, where he remained in hopes of obtaining a bishopric. He appears, in fact, to have wished to return to Britain or Ireland, though his letters show him to have been strongly opposed to any suggestion of a legislative union of the two.

MacSparran moved among the elite of the community, including rich planters and slaveowners, and in 1722 married Hannah, daughter of his wealthiest parishioner, William Gardiner of Boston Neck. Attempting unsuccessfully to arrange an American episcopate, he travelled to England (1754), where his wife died of smallpox on 24 June 1755. She was buried in Broadway chapel in Westminster. He returned to America (February 1756) and died in December 1757 in South Kingston, Rhode Island, willing his home and farm to a future American bishop. He was buried under the communion table of St Paul's. A portrait by John Smibert – there is another of his wife – is owned by Bowdoin College, Brunswick, Maine. Copies of Smibert's works were made in the latter part of the nineteenth century by Mary Anstis Updike of North Kingstown, a distant relative of MacSparran, and remain in the possession of the Rhode Island Historical Society. The portrait of his wife is in the Museum of Fine Arts, Boston.

Seán P. Donlan

SOURCES
Allibone; John Canon O'Hanlon, *Irish-American history of the United States* (1907), i, 104, 139; *Concise dictionary of American biography* (1964), 625–6; Francis Godwin James, *Ireland in the empire 1688–1770* (1973), 303–4; Michael Glazier (ed.), *The encyclopedia of the Irish in America* (1999); *ANB*

Makemie, Francis
c. 1658–1708
Presbyterian minister

Francis Makemie was born near Ramelton, Co. Donegal, and educated at Glasgow University. The presbytery of Laggan, to which he had been introduced by the Ramelton minister Thomas Drummond in January 1680 and which had overseen his studies, licensed him to preach and ordained him about late 1681. In response to a request from Col. William Stevens, the owner of Rehoboth, a plantation on the Pocomoke river, Makemie went to America in 1683. Initially he was an itinerant evangelist in Maryland, Virginia, and North Carolina, though beginning in the summer of 1684 he may have served as minister at Elizabeth River or Lynn Haven, Virginia, as suggested by his letters to Increase Mather (1639–1723), the influential minister at Massachusetts Bay. In 1687 Makemie settled in Accomack County, Virginia, where he purchased land, engaged in trade, and ministered at nearby Rehoboth. About 1689 he went to London, primarily to enlist ministers. Expanding his trade to Barbados, he purchased a house there by early 1690 and obtained a licence to preach. His involvement in the West Indies trade was probably facilitated by his association with William Anderson, a prosperous merchant and landowner in Accomack County, and Anderson's wife Mary. He married their daughter Naomi (b. *c.* 1668), sometime between 1687 and 1698. They had two daughters, Elizabeth (d. 1708) and Anne (d. 1787/8).

Makemie published his first work, a catechism, in 1691, though no copy is extant. Having read it, the Quaker George Keith visited Makemie at his home in Virginia, accused him of being a false teacher, and challenged him to a public disputation. Makemie declined, partly because he was reluctant to engage in learned debate before an ignorant crowd, but he challenged Keith to record his criticism. To this Makemie responded in *An answer to George Keith's libel*, dated 26 July 1692 but not published until 1694 at Boston, with the endorsement of Increase Mather, his son Cotton Mather, Samuel Willard, and others. In 1692 Makemie preached in Philadelphia, and in the next year or two he took up residence in Barbados. While there, he wrote *Truths in a true light*, dated 28 December 1697 but not published until 1699 at Edinburgh. In it he cited the Catholic threat and defended Protestant nonconformists as agreeing with Anglicans on all substantive matters of doctrine and sacraments, though differing in ceremonies, polity, and discipline. Persecuting Dissenters, he insisted, undermined the Protestant interest. In January 1698 he was chagrined to learn that Increase Mather's son Samuel had decided not to come to Barbados because of an outbreak of disease. Later that year Makemie returned to Virginia, though he continued to engage in commerce with Barbados.

On 8 June 1698 Makemie purchased land on the Elizabeth river in Princess Anne County, Virginia, and several months later he and his wife inherited substantial property when her father died. By 1704 he was the second largest landholder in Accomack County, with 5,109 acres. The governor of Virginia approved his request for permission to minister on 29 April 1699, and on 5 October the Accomack court issued a licence based on the one he had received in Barbados. He thus became the second licensed nonconformist minister (after the Donegal-born Josias Mackie) in the colony; he also obtained licences for his meeting-houses at Onanocok and Pocomoke. During the summer of 1704 he returned to England to recruit ministers, successfully enlisting John Hampton and George McNish. While in London he published *A plain and friendly perswasive* (1705), addressed to the residents of Virginia and Maryland, extolling the benefits of towns, where occupations are diversified, natural assets can be marketed, and social control can be maintained. He played a significant role in organising the first presbytery in America, which convened at Philadelphia in the spring of 1706 and again in December of that year; on both occasions he served as moderator.

In January 1707 Makemie and Hampton met in New York City with Lord Cornbury, governor of New York and New Jersey, and thereafter Makemie preached at a shoemaker's house in the city, as did Hampton on Long Island. For preaching without a licence they were arrested on Cornbury's orders on 23 January, and imprisoned until obtaining release on a writ of *habeas corpus* on 11 March. At his trial in June Makemie was acquitted after arguing that he had a valid licence, and that the Act of Toleration, with its licensing requirement, was in any case irrelevant because the Church of England was not established in the American colonies. Although acquitted, he was nevertheless responsible for all expenses, which exceeded £83 (including travel). He published both the sermon he had preached in New York, *A good conversation* (1707), and an account of his legal difficulties, *A narrative of … American imprisonment* (1707). Both works were printed in Boston, which he visited that summer. He and Cotton Mather went to Salem in August. He apparently did not attend the presbytery at Philadelphia in May 1708, though he was still ministering at Rehoboth in early June. Sometime between 10 June and 4 August 1708 he died, probably at Accomack. According to his will, dated 27 April 1708, he owned thirty-three slaves, substantial land, and livestock, and he had a library of approximately a thousand volumes.

Richard L. Greaves

SOURCES
E. B. O'Callaghan and B. Fernow (ed.), *Documents relative to the colonial history of the state of New-York* (15 vols, 1853–97), iii, 709; iv, 1186–7; William M. Engle (ed.), *Records of the Presbyterian Church in the United States of America: embracing the minutes of the general presbytery and general synod, 1706–1788* (1904), 9–11; H. R. McIlwaine and W. L. Hall (ed.), *Executive journals of the council of colonial Virginia* (5 vols, 1925–45), i, 427; iii, 52; Cotton Mather, *Diary of Cotton Mather*, ed. Worthington Chauncey Ford (2 vols, 1957), i, 550, 596, 599; Louis des Cognets, Jr., *English duplicates of lost Virginia records* (1958), 124; James H. Smylie, 'Francis Makemie: tradition and challenge', *Journal of Presbyterian history*, lxi (1983), 197–209; Boyd Stanley Schlenther (ed.), *The life and writings of Francis Makemie, father of American Presbyterianism (c. 1658–1708)* (1999)

Martin, William
1729?–1807?
Reformed Presbyterian minister

William Martin was born on 16 May 1729 or 1733 at Ballyspallen, near Ballykelly, Co. Londonderry, eldest son of David Martin. He had at least one sister, who was married in Scotland. William entered Glasgow University in 1750 and graduated in 1753; he studied theology in Scotland under John McMillan, founder of the Scottish Reformed Presbyterian church. In 1756 he was licensed to preach, and in 1757 he became the first minister in Ireland of the Reformed Presbyterian church when he was ordained by the Scottish presbytery (2 July 1757) in the open air at the Vow, Co. Antrim, where hundreds of adherents, from both Co. Antrim and Co. Londonderry, had been wont to meet to hear the Covenanter minister, David Houston (1633?–96). Martin preached in many places in Antrim, Londonderry, north Down, and possibly Donegal, until in 1760, when he was moderator of the Scottish presbytery, two congregations were established in Ireland, and he was made responsible for the Antrim Covenanting societies. He fixed his residence at Kellswater, near Ballymena. The area experienced economic pressures caused by increased rent demands, and by a downturn in the linen industry, and Martin decided to emigrate to America, where he seems to have hoped that it would be possible to establish a covenanted polity, and to experience enhanced civic and religious liberty. He placed an advertisement in the *Belfast News Letter* of 31 December 1771, seeking people of like mind to travel along with him, and acted as an agent for the enterprise; in July 1772 he advertised the sale of his property in Kellswater, and in September 1772 he and five shiploads of emigrants sailed from Larne to South Carolina.

He was the first Reformed Presbyterian minister in the southern states. He preached first to a Presbyterian congregation known as Catholic congregation at Rocky Creek, South Carolina, around which many Co. Antrim families continued to live in close association. Presbyterians in the back country of the Carolinas were in the forefront of the movement towards republican independence. The Sunday after what the Scotch-Irish regarded as a massacre by the British of their men at Waxhaw, South Carolina, on 29 May 1780, Martin preached an impassioned sermon, comparing the Waxhaw event to the sufferings of the Scottish Covenanters, and urging his hearers to take up arms. He was arrested the next day by British troops. After six months in prison, he was put on trial before Lord Cornwallis in Winnsboro in 1781. He is said to have testified that since the king had failed to protect the rights of his subjects, allegiance was no longer required, and that the 'Declaration of Independence is but a reiteration of what our covenanting fathers have always maintained'. As a result, the minister was sentenced to death. A Col. Philips who had known Martin in Ireland intervened at the last moment to save his life, but his meeting-house was burned. Martin took refuge for a time in Mecklenburg County, North Carolina, and returned after the revolution to preach in Catholic congregation. When the British evacuated Charleston, Martin is said to have shouted '... and may the devil go with them'.

It appears that Martin refused to join the Associate Reformed Church founded in 1782, maintaining that he was the only minister who kept alive the principles of the Reformed Presbyterian church in America. A church was built for him at Rocky Mount, but he was dismissed by his congregation in 1785 for intemperance. He continued to preach to the Covenanting societies and supplied the congregation of Long Cane. He joined two ministers from Ireland in setting up a Reformed Presbytery in 1798. He later fell out with the Reformed Presbytery, when the other two ministers were preparing to discipline him for drunkenness and for selling a negro before the enactment of the church's decree that slaves should be freed. He preached until shortly before his death, which was either on 25 October 1806 or on 13 January 1807; his death may have been caused by the effects of a fever which he suffered after a fall from his horse. He was married three times (all undated): his first wife, whose name was Mary, died in Ireland; his second was Jenny Cherry, and his third was Susanna Boggs; she survived him. A nineteenth-century account says he performed his own marriage ceremony, presumably because he did not recognise other clergy. He had had one daughter, who died before him, and he left land to three nephews, though his will was set aside on account of his confused mental condition.

Linde Lunney

SOURCES
Adam Loughridge, *Fasti of the Reformed Presbyterian Church of Ireland* (1970); Jean Stephenson, *Scotch-Irish migration to South Carolina 1772: Rev. William Martin and his five shiploads of settlers* (1971); Adam Loughridge, *The Covenanters in Ireland* (1983), 17–19, 39–40; Robert Buchanan, *Kellswater RP church Co. Antrim a short history*, ed. Eull Dunlop (1989); Billy Kennedy, *The Scots-Irish in the hills of Tennessee* (1995); 'Back of historic map of Fairfield (Legend)' (www.rootsweb.com/~scfairfi/legend.html (downloaded Aug. 2002)); Sam Thomas, 'The 1780 Presbyterian rebellion and the battle of Huck's Defeat' (www.yorkcounty.org/brattonsvile/Huck/1780-Huck.html; (downloaded Aug. 2002)); *'The Belfast Newsletter index'* (www.ucs.louisiana.edu/bnl/); Linda Merle, 'Five ships to Carolina and the Rev. Martin' (http://homepages.rootsweb.com/~merle/Rm/ (downloaded Aug. 2002)); Phyllis Bauer, 'References to the Linn/Lynns in the Draper manuscripts, with a brief description of the content as found in the Calendar of the Thomas Sumter Papers' (www.lynn-linn-lineage-quarterly.com/Draper/Sumpter%?OPapers.htm (downloaded Aug. 2002)); James H. Lynn, 'County Antrim Ireland to Chester county, South Carolina to Randolph county, Illinois' (www.rootsweb.com/~ilrandol/earlysettlers6.html#_edn2 (downloaded Aug. 2002)); information from Rebekah J. Wilson of Washington State, USA; information from Linda Smetzer

Montgomery, Richard
1738–75
Soldier

Richard Montgomery was born on 2 December 1738 at Feltrim, near Swords, Co. Dublin, third son of three sons and one daughter of Thomas Montgomery (*c.* 1700–61), MP for Lifford, Co. Donegal (1729–60), and Mary Montgomery (née Franklin). His elder brother was Capt. Alexander Montgomery (1720–1800), MP for Co. Donegal (1768–1800). Richard was educated at St Andrew's school before entering Trinity College Dublin on 15 June 1754. In 1756 he left Trinity without a degree and was commissioned (21 September) as an ensign in the 17th Foot. He served in North America during the Seven Years' War (1756–63) and was present at the siege of Louisbourg (July 1758) under Gen. Wolfe, was promoted to lieutenant (10 July 1759), and took part in the attack on the French forts on Lake Champlain (1759). In 1760 he was appointed adjutant of his regiment and was present at the capture of Montreal. He later served in the campaign to capture Martinique (1762), took part in the siege of Havana, Cuba, and was promoted to captain (May 1762). At the end of the war he was stationed in New York, returning to England in 1765. During his time in England he moved in political circles and was acquainted with prominent whigs such as Isaac Barré, Charles James Fox, and Edmund Burke.

Frustrated at not being promoted to major, he sold his commission in April 1772 and moved to New York some months later. Planning to live as a gentleman farmer, he bought a farm near King's Bridge, thirteen miles north of New York city. In July 1773 he married Janet Livingston, whom he had met eight years before, the daughter of Judge Robert R. Livingston, and spent the first few years of his marriage at his wife's residence near Rhinebeck, New York. They had no children. The Livingston family held strong pro-colonial views and Montgomery came to support the American cause, being elected in May 1775 to represent Dutchess County in the New York Provincial Congress. Owing to his previous military experience he was appointed a brigadier-general in the American Continental army on 22 June 1775, an appointment he accepted with some reluctance. Acting as second-in-command to Gen. Philip Schuyler, he served during the invasion of Canada and was present during the siege operations against St John's and Chambly on the Richelieu river.

In September 1775 Schuyler resigned his command due to illness and Montgomery took command of the army, capturing St John's and Chambly on 19 October. These were the first successes for the American army during the revolutionary war, and on 11 November he seized Montreal after its evacuation by the British. On 2 December he rendezvous-ed with Gen. Benedict Arnold, and the combined army laid siege to Quebec. On the morning of 31 December 1775 the two generals led their men in an unsuccessful assault on the city, under cover of a heavy snowstorm. Montgomery's men faltered when they reached a blockhouse at Cape Diamond on the outskirts of Quebec, and he was killed by artillery fire while trying to encourage them forward. His body was later recognised by officers of the British garrison and he was buried with full honours. He had been promoted to major-general on 9 December but had not received the news.

News of his death was greeted with scenes of regret in New York, Philadelphia, and London, where both Burke and Fox commented in the House of Commons on his death. A monument was erected to his memory in St Paul's church in New York, and in 1818 his remains were returned to New York and reinterred in St Paul's. A memorial plaque was also placed at Cape Diamond where he died. There are substantial collections of his letters in the New York Public Library, the Library of Congress, and the New-York Historical Society. He has also been the subject of several biographies, including Hal T. Shelton, *General Richard Montgomery and the American revolution* (1994).

David Murphy

SOURCES
Army List, 1762; *Gentleman's Magazine*, Jan. 1776, 39; Feb. 1776, 91–2; *Annual Register, 1776*; Webb; *DNB*; *Appletons*; *Alumni Dublinensis* (1935); Hal T. Shelton, *General Richard Montgomery and the American revolution* (1994); *DAB*; *DCB*; E. M. Johnston-Liik (ed.), *History of the Irish parliament 1692–1800* (6 vols, 2002) v, 286

Moylan, Stephen
1734?–1811
Soldier in the US army

Stephen Moylan was born in Co. Cork, son of John Moylan, a prominent Catholic merchant. His father, socially restricted by the penal laws, was obliged to send his four sons to Paris for a Catholic education. While Stephen's brother Francis (1735–1815) studied for the priesthood and later became bishop successively of Kerry and Cork, he and his remaining brothers, Jasper and John, made careers in America. Initially, Stephen worked in Lisbon and London to establish himself in the shipping business, a first step towards his career in the American revolutionary elite. Dealing in transatlantic trade he made important east-coast connections, especially in Philadelphia, where he settled in 1768, joined by his brothers. On 17 March 1771 at Miller's Tavern in the city waterfront area, Moylan became a founder member and president of the Society of the Friendly Sons of St Patrick. His organisation was a non-sectarian philanthropic club, providing relief aid for ill and destitute Irish immigrants.

Socially and politically influential, Moylan and his circle were quick to infiltrate the emergent revolutionary movement which in 1775 broke into active insurrection against Great Britain. They fully participated in the revolutionary war at the highest level. One of his fellow Friendly Sons, Commodore John Barry of Wexford (future 'father of the American navy') joined the war at sea; Moylan set his sights on the army. Recommended by his friend John Dickinson, who drafted the 'olive-branch petition' (1775) and early drafts of the US articles of confederation (1777), he gained appointment as muster-master general in August 1775. One of his main responsibilities was to supply American privateers in the sea war against the British. The commander-in-chief, George Washington noted Moylan's ability and self-assurance, and ordered Moylan's transfer to his staff as secretary and ADC in March 1776. In the following June Moylan was promoted to quartermaster-general of the army on Washington's personal recommendation. Simultaneously, while Moylan's brother Jasper practised law in Philadelphia, John Moylan held the revolutionary post of clothier-general, an occupation of doubtless financial benefit in the supply of uniform and accessories for the war effort.

For the Moylans, everything depended on a successful war. In September 1776, frustrated at his failure to reorganise and equip the ill-experienced army into a force fit to withstand British advances, Stephen Moylan gave up his position in favour of his predecessor, Thomas Mifflin. On Washington's request he raised the 'independent' 1st Pennsylvania Cavalry Regiment, which, as its founder, he commanded in the field. He continued in command when it was renamed the 4th Regiment of Continental Light Dragoons. Court-martialled in October 1777 for clashing with the cavalry's Polish senior commander, Casimir Pulaski, he was exonerated and resumed his command. Moylan succeeded to Pulaski's post in March 1778 (while officially retaining command of his own regiment) and successfully led the somewhat depleted cavalry through the remainder of the war. He wintered at Valley Forge, Pennsylvania, in 1777–8, an ordeal of privation and discontent in the ranks, after which intensive spring training reinvigorated the demoralised Continental army. In 1779–80 he campaigned along the Hudson river and in Connecticut. He served later in the southern campaign, seemingly without his original regiment, and was at Yorktown in October 1781 when Washington decisively defeated Lord Cornwallis. Moylan ultimately reached the brevet rank of brigadier-general on the eve of his retirement from the military, following the war's official conclusion at the Treaty of Paris in September 1783. In spite of his early setbacks he retained his favourable relationship with Washington who (as an elected member) was present at the 1782 New Year dinner of the Friendly Sons of St Patrick, hosted in his honour for the victory of Yorktown, and at the March anniversary dinner.

On leaving the army in November 1783, Moylan returned to his civilian career as a Philadelphia merchant, possibly disappointed at his relative lack of share in military glory. He was a naturally good-humoured man and made a happy home life in Pennsylvania, having married (September 1778) Mary Ricketts Van Horn, a merchant's daughter from Phil's Hill, New

Jersey. He remained in the thoughts of Washington, who as first US president appointed Moylan commissioner of loans in Philadelphia in 1793, a year after he had become registrar and recorder of Chester County. Elected to a second term as president of the Friendly Sons of St Patrick in 1796, Stephen Moylan died on 13 April 1811 in Philadelphia and was buried at the Catholic churchyard of St Mary's.

Patrick Long

SOURCES

Freeman's Journal, 11 July 1811; *Dublin Evening Post*, 20 July 1811; *Appletons*; John J. Delaney and James Edward Tobin, *Dictionary of Catholic biography* (1962); Mark Mayo Boatner, *Cassell's biographical dictionary of the American War of Independence* (1966); *Who was who in America: historical volume 1607–1896* (1967); *Cork Historical Society Journal*, lxxxiii (1978), 63; Michael F. Funchion, *Irish American voluntary organizations* (1983); *Who was who in the American revolution* (1993); Michael Glazier (ed.), *The encyclopedia of the Irish in America* (1999)

O'Donel, James Louis
1737–1811
First Catholic bishop of Newfoundland

James Louis O'Donel was born near Knocklofty, Co. Tipperary, son of Michael O'Donel and Ann O'Donel (née Crosby), well-to-do farmers. Initially tutored privately, James was later sent to Limerick for classical studies. He probably joined the Franciscans in Limerick, went to Boulay in France to begin his studies and then to St Isidore's College in Rome, where he was ordained priest in 1761. (He had at least one brother, Michael (d. 1790), also a Franciscan.) Afterwards James taught theology and philosophy in Prague and served as a chaplain to several distinguished families before returning to Ireland in 1768. In 1770 he became guardian of the Franciscan friary in Clonmel until 1776. In that year he was elected a provincial definitor, served as provincial (1779–82), and was appointed guardian of the Waterford friary.

During the course of the eighteenth century increasing numbers of people from Ireland, a large proportion of whom came from the Waterford area, worked in the fisheries and settled in Newfoundland. On 14 January 1784, with restrictions against Catholic worship eased, allowing a chapel to be built and marriage services to be performed, four Irishmen from Waterford wrote to William Egan (1726–96), bishop of Waterford, on behalf of the Catholic community in Newfoundland, requesting that a priest with the authority to regularise services be sent to St John's; they specifically asked for O'Donel, a Recollet priest, who was known as a popular preacher and an Irish-speaker. Bishop Egan forwarded the letter, together with supporting documents, to Bishop James Talbot of London, who was then responsible for Newfoundland and who authorised O'Donel to go as vicar general to the Newfoundland mission. However, he also sent the letter and documents to the cardinals of the Sacred Congregation of Propaganda Fide, who on 17 May appointed O'Donel superior of the mission. On 30 May 1784 Pope Pius VI appointed O'Donel prefect apostolic of the new ecclesiastical territory of Newfoundland, directly under the jurisdiction of Propaganda Fide. O'Donel arrived in St John's on 4 July 1784, where he began work by obtaining authority to build a chapel. Within six years he had sent away several unauthorised clergy and, with the assistance of Archbishop John Thomas Troy of Dublin, brought out Irish-speaking priests to minister to the missions at the newly built chapels in Placentia, Harbour Grace, and Ferryland, with the result that the Catholic community in Newfoundland grew and prospered. Both the clergy and laity appealed to Pope Pius VI to make O'Donel a bishop, and on 23 December 1795 he was appointed titular bishop of Thyatira *in partibus infidelium* and appointed vicar apostolic of Newfoundland. The following 21 September 1796 O'Donel was consecrated the first English-speaking Catholic bishop in British North America at a ceremony in Quebec by Bishop Jean-François Hubert.

In a time of revolution and turbulence in North America, Europe, and Ireland, Bishop O'Donel was politically cautious and loyal to the crown. Both the excesses and the ideology of the French revolution alarmed him and he found offensive the sight of French prisoners of war attending church services with cockades on their hats, 'large emblems of infidelity and rebellion', he told Archbishop Troy of Dublin. He was more comfortable with Irish troops marching to church, even under the command of Protestant officers. When in 1799 he learned of a plot by United Irishmen, both within his parish and within the Newfoundland Regiment of Fencibles, to overthrow the colonial government, O'Donel warned the commanding officer, Col. John Skerrett, and counselled obedience to his flock, thus foiling the plan. A second United Irishmen rebellion was planned in 1800 within the fencibles, but it too was discovered and thwarted. In the diocesan statutes of the following year (1801) he urged his priests to 'inculcate a willing obedience to the salutary laws of England, and to the commands of the governor and magistrates of this island'. He also directed that prayers be said each Sunday for King George III and the royal family. Bishop O'Donel established good relations with many of the Protestant religious leaders of the Newfoundland community and with many of the merchants and colonial administrators. When the Irish Benevolent Society was founded in 1806 for the relief of the poor, largely by Protestant Irishmen, O'Donel was pleased to be its patron. He also maintained friendly relations with his fellow bishops in Quebec and Ireland.

Bishop O'Donel worked hard to promote good relations between his Irish Catholic flock and the largely English Protestant colonial administration. There were occasional setbacks in his largely successful efforts. Rear-admiral John Elliott and Governor Mark Milbanke wanted to restrict the activities of priests and discourage Irish Catholic settlement in Newfoundland. In a celebrated incident in 1786, Prince William Henry, duke of Clarence, while serving in the Royal Navy in Newfoundland, got into an altercation with O'Donel in St John's and threw an iron file at him; O'Donel went into hiding until the prince, to the relief of everyone including the colonial governor, returned to sea duty. Bishop O'Donel's services in promoting stability within the Irish Catholic community were gradually recognised by the colonial administration. Col. Skerrett and others sought a pension for O'Donel in 1800 and the merchants and leading citizens of St John's similarly appealed to the governor in 1804, with the result that the bishop was given a pension of £50 per year.

With his health beginning to fail, Bishop O'Donel asked the Holy See for a successor. In August 1806 an Irish Franciscan, Patrick Lambert, arrived in St John's to be bishop coadjutor with the right of succession; O'Donel resigned on 1 January 1807. Both the Catholic and Protestant communities paid homage to O'Donel before he left. An extravagant dinner was given for him by the leading figures in St John's and the merchants contributed to the purchase of a silver cup, valued at 150 guineas (£157 10s.). O'Donel sailed for Ireland in July and retired to a Franciscan friary in Waterford. There several years later he fell asleep while reading and a candle ignited the chair in which he was sitting. Although he was not seriously injured, the shock was such that he died several days later on 15 April 1811. Remembered as 'the apostle of Newfoundland', Bishop O'Donel built the Catholic church in Newfoundland in the aftermath of the penal era.

Francis M. Carroll

SOURCES

Archives of the archdiocese of Dublin, Troy papers; Archives of the archdiocese of St John's (Newfoundland), Howley papers; Archives of the Sacred Congregation 'de Propaganda Fide' (Rome); TNA, CO 5/470–506, CO 194/35–44, WO 1/15; 'The first bishop of Newfoundland', *Irish Ecclesiastical Record*, ii (1866), 508–23; M. F. Howley, *Ecclesiastical history of Newfoundland* (1888; repr. 1979); *DCB*; *DNB*; Philip O'Connell, 'Dr James Louis O'Donnell (1737–1811), first bishop of Newfoundland', *Irish Ecclesiastical Record*, ciii (1965), 308–24; Cyril J. Byrne (ed.), *Gentlemen-bishops and faction fighters* (1984); Terence J. Fay, *A history of Canadian Catholics: Gallicanism, Romanism, and Canadianism* (2002)

Paterson, William
1745–1806
Lawyer, attorney general and governor of New Jersey, and US supreme court judge

William Paterson was born on 24 December 1745, probably in Antrim town, Co. Antrim (though some sources say he was born at sea), the eldest son among three sons and two daughters of Richard Paterson and his wife Mary (d. 1772). The Patersons emigrated (1747) to New Castle, Delaware, and, after living in New York and Connecticut, settled (1750) in Princeton, New Jersey. They were most probably related to a Paterson family from Ireland, who founded an important tin manufactory in Berlin, Connecticut, in 1740, said to have been the first in America. It is known that Richard Paterson worked in tinplate manufacture and peddled tin wares; he later established a general store in Princeton, in which his son worked for a time.

Princeton offered young William the opportunity for an excellent education: first at local schools, including the Latin school founded by Aaron Burr, and then at the College of New Jersey (Princeton) where he enrolled (1759) and took his BA (1763) and MA (1766). He was a keen student of history and moral philosophy. Paterson helped found the Well Meaning Club in the college *c.* 1765, and in 1770 reestablished it as the Cliosophic Society, the country's oldest political, literary, and debating society. In the year after the enactment of the stamp act (1765), Paterson delivered the commencement speech, entitled 'Patriotism', at his MA conferring. He served as trustee of Princeton (1787–1802). While Paterson pursued his graduate degree, he studied law with Richard Stockton, a leading Princeton attorney who later signed the declaration of independence. Admitted to the New Jersey bar (1769), Paterson started to practise law in Hunterdon and Somerset counties, but had to supplement his modest income by keeping a shop. Though he wrote to a college friend that he wished to live an easy life without much bustle, he was to become a principal player in state and national government. Conservative and cautious by nature, he appears to have been hesitant to join the revolutionary cause. When he did, his actions were informed by his interest in moral philosophy.

Paterson was a delegate from Somerset County to the first Provincial Congress (1775–6), and became its secretary. He continued as secretary in the second and third Congresses, attending to all the correspondence between the Provincial Congress and the Continental Congress, as well as recording the congressional deliberations. He twice turned down the opportunity to be a member of the Continental Congress (1778, 1781). Paterson was attorney general of New Jersey in 1776–83 and was elected to the New Jersey legislative council (1776–7) and to the council of safety (1777), under whose authority he prosecuted loyalists and war profiteers. In his work with the legislative council, as in his later roles, he recognised the importance of maintaining existing local governance, particularly the county court system.

Paterson returned to his increasingly successful law practice in 1783, but led the New Jersey delegation to the constitutional convention in 1787. He emerged as an important player in the proceedings because of the New Jersey (or 'Paterson') plan that he co-wrote, which was designed to protect the rights of small states. It prevailed against the 'Virginia plan', developed by James Madison, which gave the advantage to the larger states. He worked with tact and tenacity for the 'great compromise' that recognised the larger states' claim for representation based on population in the house of representatives, while it protected the interests of smaller states by establishing an upper house, the senate, with two delegates from each state. Given his work creating the shape of the Congress, it was appropriate that Paterson was elected in 1789 to represent New Jersey in the US senate; he served from 4 March 1789 until 13 November 1790. He helped his friend Senator Oliver Ellsworth, later first chief justice of the supreme court, to draft the judiciary act of 1789 which established the federal court system, an early test of the balance of power between states and the federal government.

Paterson was twice elected governor of New Jersey. He succeeded William Livingston in 1791 and served until 1793, when he was appointed to the federal bench. While governor, he codified the state's laws, some of which were based on English common law and some passed by the New Jersey legislature after independence; his codification was published as *Laws of the state of New Jersey* (1800). He also revised the rules and practices of the chancery and common law courts.

George Washington appointed Paterson associate justice of the US supreme court in March 1793; he served until 1806. As well as sitting in court in New York, he had to go on circuit, travelling thousands of miles in often difficult conditions. Among the cases he heard were those of the whiskey rebels in 1794 and *Vanhorne's Lessee* v. *Dorrance* (1795), a case involving the principle of judicial review that anticipated the landmark *Marbury* v. *Madison* (1803), with which he was also involved. In the course of his judicial career Paterson had the unusual opportunity to put to the test the judiciary act of 1789, which he had himself drafted. He was a strong constitutionalist, and supported Alexander Hamilton, the federalist secretary of the treasury.

In his last years his contribution to government and the law were recognised with honorary degrees from his alma mater, the College of New Jersey, and from Dartmouth College (1805); Harvard gave him an honorary degree in 1806. By the end of his career, Paterson was a wealthy man, with large landholdings. In 1803 a carriage accident seriously affected his health, and in 1806 he set off to take the waters at Ballston Spa, New York. He stopped en route near Albany, New York, to visit his daughter Cornelia Van Rensselaer, married into one of the wealthiest families in the country, and died on 9 September 1806 at her home. He was buried first in the Van Rensselaer family grave in the grounds of their estate; his body was later reinterred in the rural cemetery at Menands, near Albany.

Paterson married (apparently on 9 February 1779) Cornelia, daughter of a wealthy landowner, John Bell of Somerset County; they had a son and two daughters, one of whom died as an infant, before Cornelia's death in childbirth in October 1783. Two years later he married Euphemia White, who had been his first wife's best friend; there is no record of any children from the second marriage. The town of Paterson, New Jersey, founded in 1791 as an industrial site on the Great Falls of the Passaic River by the Society for Establishing Useful Manufactures, was named in honour of William Paterson. A college in Paterson was renamed William Paterson College in 1967, and became William Paterson University in 1997. There is an unsigned portrait that depicts a delicate-looking Paterson in profile, wearing his judicial robe, in the supreme court collection in Washington, DC. Paterson's papers are held in the Princeton University Library, the Library of Congress, the Rutgers University Library, and the William Paterson University Library.

Maureen Murphy

SOURCES
Appletons; Gertrude Wood, *William Paterson of New Jersey 1745–1806* (1933); Richard Haskett, 'William Paterson, attorney general of New Jersey: public office and private profit in the American Revolution', *William and Mary Quarterly*, 3rd ser., vii (1950), 26–38; Richard Haskett, 'William Paterson, counsellor at law' (Ph.D. dissertation, Princeton, 1952); Robert Schuyler, *The constitution of the United States* (1952), 75; Alexander Leitch, *A Princeton companion* (1978); John E. O'Connor, *William Paterson: lawyer and statesman 1745–1806* (1979); Andrew C. Flaviano and Charles E. Hickox, 'William Paterson: an Irishman's influence on the American judicial system', *Northern Ireland Legal Quarterly*, xli, no. 4 (1990), 352–8; Steve Ickringill, 'William Paterson, 1745–1806: lawyer and politician', G. O'Brien and P. Roebuck (ed.), *Nine Ulster lives* (1992), 111–24; *Who was who in the American revolution* (1993); Michael Glazier (ed.), *The encyclopedia of the Irish in America* (1999); *ANB*; www.familysearch.org (accessed Oct. 2007).

Penn, William
1644–1718
Quaker leader and founder of Pennsylvania

William Penn was born on 14 October 1644 in London, the elder of two sons (there was also a daughter) of William Penn (1621–70), a naval commander, and his wife, Margaret Penn (née Jasper) (1610?–1682). Penn's mother was the daughter of John Jasper, a Rotterdam merchant, and had been previously married, before 1631, to Nicholas Vanderschuren (d. 1641 or 1642), a Dutch merchant. She lived in Kilrush, Co. Clare, till the rebellion of 1641, when she fled to London. Penn senior had his first naval appointment in 1644, on a ship of the parliament's Irish fleet, whose rear-admiral he became in 1649. After 1654 his sympathies appear to have been with the exiled Charles Stuart. From 1656 to 1660 he lived with his family at Macroom Castle, Co. Cork, on estates confiscated from the MacCarthys and granted to him in 1653.

William Penn junior began to attend Chigwell Grammar School in Essex about 1653, but went to Ireland with his father in 1656. A travelling Quaker preacher, Thomas Loe, was invited by Admiral Penn to address his household in Macroom in 1657, and both Penn senior and junior appear to have been deeply impressed by him. Admiral Penn returned to England in March 1660, and met and was knighted by the returning Charles II off the Dutch coast in May 1660. The commission appointing Lord Broghill as lord president of Munster in the same month named Penn as one of his council. Sir William, however, probably did not visit Ireland again; he was elected to the English House of Commons and appointed a navy commissioner.

The younger Penn entered Christ Church College, Oxford, in 1660 but was expelled for religious non-conformity in 1662. He then went to France, and in 1663 was studying theology under Moses Amyraut at the Protestant academy at Saumur. He returned to London in 1664, and entered Lincoln's Inn in 1665, in which year he was also with the English fleet and at Whitehall. In February 1666 the twenty-one-year-old Penn was dispatched to Ireland to attend to his father's interests in new land settlement then being imposed on the kingdom. The Macroom estates had been restored to the MacCarthys, and the Act of Settlement (1662) compensated Penn with about 7,500 Irish acres, some in the barony of Ibaune and Barryroe in west Co. Cork, and more in the barony of Imokilly in east Co. Cork, with a house at Shanagarry. The young Penn, heir to an Irish estate and intended by his father for the life of a courtier, moved freely among the powerful and wealthy in Ireland. When the lord lieutenant, the duke of Ormond, went to quell a mutiny in Carrickfergus in May 1666, he was accompanied by Penn, who distinguished himself serving under Ormond's son, the earl of

Arran. Ormond's desire to make the younger Penn captain of a company of foot in place of Sir William was thwarted by the father's unwillingness to resign his command. Penn stayed in Dublin with Sir William Petty, and dealt with Sir Edward Dering, who was a member of the court of claims.

At some point in the summer or autumn of 1667 Penn encountered the Quaker Thomas Loe again in Cork and took those first steps towards becoming a Quaker that were so momentous for his future career. In November 1667 he was arrested at a Quaker meeting in Cork on the orders of the city's mayor. Penn appealed to Broghill, now earl of Orrery, who politely reminded him that the mayor was following the law and informed Sir William in England. Penn returned to England in November 1667 to face his father, who was horrified by his son's decision to embrace a religion that promised to blight his prospects in the world. Penn's commitment to his new beliefs only deepened and became more public; he published his first religious tracts in 1668 and was imprisoned in the Tower of London for blasphemy from December 1668 to July 1669.

In September 1669 Penn set out for Ireland to make new leases with his father's tenants, settle accounts in Kinsale, and, above all, to visit fellow Quakers. He met Quaker leaders such as William Edmundson and John Burnyeat, spoke at Quaker meetings, and addressed the lord lieutenant, Lord Robartes, and the privy council on behalf of Quakers, who were being persecuted by the authorities; his lobbying of the council was inconclusive at first. He also engaged in theological disputations with Protestants and Catholics and – a sign of his growing confidence – on occasion rebuffed hostile interruptions at Quaker meetings. He mingled with Co. Cork grandees such as Robert Southwell, Sir John Brodrick, and the Boyles, and formed an association with Col. Robert Phaire. On returning to Dublin he had meetings with Lord Berkeley, the new viceroy, and (more remarkably) the lord chancellor, Archbishop Michael Boyle; he again addressed the privy council, which now ordered the release of imprisoned Quakers. He left Ireland in August 1670, having cemented enduring friendships among the Quakers there.

Penn, who had written more tracts while in Ireland, continued to publish and campaign on behalf of Quakers on his return to England. His talents, together with his social standing and the Irish estates he inherited on his father's death in 1670, gave him access to the politically powerful that no other Quaker enjoyed. He began to work with a pioneering lobbying body, the 'meeting for sufferings', established by English Quakers in 1675. In 1678 he became involved in whig politics, and allied himself with the republican Algernon Sidney. Despite these affiliations he enjoyed good relations with Charles II and his brother James, duke of York, who had worked closely with Sir William Penn. Penn was drawn into colonial affairs in 1674 when he was asked to arbitrate in a dispute between two Quakers in the colony of New Jersey, and in 1680 he petitioned the king to be allowed to establish his own colony. Having failed to achieve religious toleration in England, he hoped to establish a tolerant commonwealth. He also – as financial management was never one of his talents – needed a new source of income. In 1680, on the day he received his charter for Pennsylvania, he wrote to Robert Turner, a Dublin cloth merchant, explaining that he would have preferred not to have the name 'Penn' incorporated in the name of the colony – 'I feared least it should be looked on as a vanity in me' – but that the king insisted on it in honour of Sir William (*Papers of William Penn*, ii, 83). He immediately began to recruit Irish purchasers, mainly but not exclusively Quaker, of land in Pennsylvania. It has been estimated that Irish Quaker migration to Pennsylvania between 1682 and 1750 amounted to 440 adults, whose departure must have had a considerable impact on the Quaker community in Ireland. Penn wrote in 1684 to Arran, then Irish lord deputy, pleading for Irish Quakers and eulogising Pennsylvania. Arran assured him of his care for Quakers, and asserted that Penn's letter was 'so well writ that I should have ordered the printing of it, if I did not fear that the description you make of that place would invite so many from hence as to do prejudice to this country, which wants people in proportion as much as yours does' (*Papers of William Penn*, ii, 589).

Penn spent the years 1682–4 in Pennsylvania, establishing its government and disputing its boundaries with governors of neighbouring colonies, including Thomas Dongan of New York. He intended to return, but a visit to England was prolonged indefinitely by the accession of James II in 1685. The new king, Penn's friend, was moving towards a policy of religious toleration and Penn found himself representing not simply the Quaker interest but Protestant Dissenters in general. His influence was such that, in September 1688, when a group of Irish Protestants were seeking a friend at court to represent their case to James, it was to Penn that they addressed their appeal. There is insufficient evidence to show whether he influenced James's Irish policy. It is notable, however, that, although Irish Quakers – like other Protestants – reported heavy losses during James's reign, the Jacobite parliament of 1689 did not name Penn or other prominent Quakers in its Act of Attainder.

The extent of Penn's loyalty to James after William of Orange had assumed the English crown remains controversial. Penn was tainted, however, and suffered complete political eclipse for several years, enduring imprisonment, periods spent in hiding, charges of treason, and exclusion from the government of Pennsylvania. Eventually his friend Viscount Sidney, with the earls of Ranelagh and Rochester (qv), obtained the king's pardon for him in December 1693. Old political friendships were now revived, and new ones formed. As always, Irishmen as well as Englishmen involved in the government of Ireland were prominent among these associates. By the late 1690s Penn was again a figure whose influence was sought, as in 1697 when Richard Coote, earl of Bellomont, asked for his support in lobbying the government.

In May 1698 he went to Ireland: his purposes, as usual, included estate business and the Quaker ministry, but he also wished to quash the indictment for treason made against him in Dublin in 1691 by the disgraced spy William Fuller. On landing in Dublin, Penn published (with assistance from Anthony Sharp, among others) a Quaker tract, and two more followed shortly after. The bishop of Cork, Edward Wetenhall, was stung into publishing a rejoinder, and a pamphlet controversy between the two continued after Penn's return to England in November 1698. In the matter of the indictment, he was received with great courtesy by the Irish lords justices, the marquis of Winchester (later the 2nd duke of Bolton) and the earl of Galway. Finding the country exercised by the prospect of an English ban on Irish woollen imports, he penned a memorandum to the lords justices on the state of Ireland. His proposals included a heavy tax on the estates of absentee landowners, of whom he was of course one. He travelled with his son and with Thomas Story, a rising English Quaker. In New Ross, under a recent act forbidding Catholics to own horses worth more than £5, the Quaker party suffered seizure of their horses by unscrupulous army officers, who knew that their objection to oaths would prevent them swearing that they were not 'papists'. Penn used his influence to obtain swift redress from the government in Dublin. A few years after Penn's visit, a new Irish Quaker committee was established to lobby against laws adversely affecting Quakers. While there is no direct evidence of Penn's inspiration, the committee was closely modelled on the English Quaker meeting for sufferings, and among its members were many of Penn's Irish friends.

He never made another Irish visit, though he continued to contemplate one and retained a strong emotional tie to Quakers in Ireland. His remaining active years were largely taken up with troubles in Pennsylvania, but even here Irish-born associates often appeared, notably his capable secretary James Logan. Money troubles later overwhelmed Penn, and his imprisonment for debt in 1708 was ended in part by loans raised by Irish Quakers. His powers were by now in decline, and he never recovered from a series of strokes in 1712. He died on 30 July 1718 at his home in Ruscombe, near Twyford in Berkshire.

He married first, in 1673, Gulielma Springett (d. 1694), daughter of Sir William Springett, of Sussex, a parliamentary officer, and his wife, Mary, daughter of Sir John Proude. Three of the four daughters from this marriage died young, and only one of their sons, William, survived his father; William inherited the English and Irish estates. Penn married secondly, in 1696, Hannah, daughter of Thomas Callowhill, a merchant in Bristol; there was one surviving daughter and four sons from this marriage.

John Bergin

SOURCES
Albert Cook Myers, *Immigration of the Irish Quakers into Pennsylvania, 1682–1750; with their early history in Ireland* (1902; repr. 1969); Mary M. Dunn and Richard S. Dunn (ed.), *The papers of William Penn* (5 vols, 1981–7); Nicholas Canny, 'The Irish background to Penn's experiment', *The world of William Penn*, ed. Mary M. Dunn and Richard S. Dunn (1986); Mary K. Geiter, *William Penn* (2000); J. Bergin, 'The Quaker lobby and its influence on Irish legislation, 1692–1705', *Eighteenth-Century Ireland*, 19 (2004), 9–36

Pollock, Oliver
c. 1737–1823
Financier and revolutionary in America

Oliver Pollock was born in Ireland; he grew up in Bready, Co. Tyrone, second son of Jared Pollock. In 1760 he emigrated to Carlisle, Pennsylvania, with his father and older brother, and settled there for two years. Moving to Philadelphia, he became a successful sea-captain and merchant and established lucrative links with a leading trading house in Havana, Cuba. After engaging in a profitable commerce with the West Indies in slaves, foodstuffs, and general utensils, he moved to the lower Mississippi valley in 1768 and used his connections with Gen. Alejandro O'Reilly to avoid trade restrictions. Investing his enormous profits, he purchased (1772) a plantation at Tunica Bend, north of Baton Rouge.

With the outbreak of the American War of Independence in 1775 he immediately threw his support behind the revolutionary cause. His financial power was considerable and he channelled his funds into making New Orleans a suitable base of operations in the west. Impressed at his ability to secure shipments of gunpowder and arms, in 1777 the Continental Congress named him its commercial agent in New Orleans. Jumping at this opportunity with great enthusiasm, Pollock took part in various raids on British settlements along the Mississippi and used his own money to help finance the campaign. Around this time (1 April 1778) Pollock is credited with creating the '$' symbol for the new American currency. Through his friendship with the governor of Louisiana he also secured Spanish support for his military endeavours; this proved significant when it came to securing advances, totalling almost $300,000, for both the Continental Congress and the state of Virginia (for whom he was also acting as agent). Unfortunately for Pollock, his exuberance cost him his fortune. By 1781 all his money was gone and the loans he had helped negotiate were recalled. He travelled to Philadelphia to help persuade the Congress and Virginia to honour their commitments, but they reneged on their promises and he was left bankrupt. It took over thirty years for him finally to receive full compensation for what he was owed. Moving to Cuba in 1783, he briefly served as commercial representative of the new United States, before being arrested and imprisoned for debt. Returning to Carlisle, and then New Orleans (1787), he spent the next years rebuilding his fortune, partly through a profitable trade in slaves. Becoming involved in politics, he ran unsuccessfully for election to the house of representatives as a federalist candidate for Cumberland County, Pennsylvania, in 1804. After this, he decided to settle in Baltimore, Maryland, where he used his Caribbean expertise to run a merchant house specialising in trade with Cuba and the other islands.

He married first (1765) Margaret O'Brien (d. 1799) at Havana, Cuba; they had five sons and three daughters. He married secondly (1805) a widow, Winifred Deady. There were legal difficulties when she died in 1814: her children from her first marriage laid claim to part of his estate, and Pollock was so disillusioned that he moved to live with one of his daughters in Pinckneyville, Mississippi. He died there on 17 December 1823. Although Pollock is considered a minor and somewhat shadowy figure, his support for the revolutionary struggle in the west is recognised as decisive. Without his timely supplies to the campaigns of George Rogers Clark, in particular, it is likely that the entire north-west would have been lost to the new United States. Despite his harsh treatment by Congress, he never complained or lost faith in it as a political institution. This, as much as his work as a financier in the west, has ensured his high reputation as a patriot of the revolutionary period.

Patrick M. Geoghegan

SOURCES
James Alton James, 'Oliver Pollock, financier of the American revolution in the west', *Studies: an Irish Quarterly Review*, xviii (1929), 633–47; id., 'Oliver Pollock and the free navigation of the Mississippi River', *Mississippi Valley Historical Review*, xix, no. 3 (1932), 331–47; id., *Oliver Pollock: the life and times of an unknown patriot* (1937); Light Townsend Cummins, *Spanish observers and the American revolution, 1775–83* (1992); *Who was who in the American revolution* (1993); *ANB*

Ramage, John
1746–1802
Miniaturist and goldsmith

John Ramage was born in Dublin, and entered the Dublin Society's schools in 1763. He married Elizabeth, daughter of Henry Liddell, a London merchant, prior to his emigration to Canada; they had two children, John and Elizabeth Ramage. He was a resident of Halifax, Nova Scotia (1772–4), and then lived in Boston prior to the American revolution. According to church records from Trinity church, Boston, Massachusetts, on 8 March 1776 John Ramage was married for the second time, possibly bigamously, to Maria Victoria Ball.

Ramage was a Protestant, and was on the loyalist side in the war. While in Boston, owing to his tory affiliations Ramage received most of his commissions from officers of the British army and tory families, which may explain why his paintings (as portable miniatures) are not found in Boston. He received a commission as a lieutenant in the Loyal Irish Volunteers, a loyalist regiment formed in 1775 for the defence of Boston under Capt. James Forrest. In the spring of 1776 he accompanied Gen. Howe's army as it withdrew from Boston, at which time he returned to Halifax, Canada. His third marriage (*c.* 1776) was to a Mrs Taylor, in St Paul's church, Halifax. This was almost certainly a bigamous marriage (although it is possible that Mrs Taylor was in fact his first wife Elizabeth), and Maria Victoria Ramage divorced him in or around 1779. It was to escape prosecution for bigamy and debt that in 1777 Ramage and his wife left Halifax and settled in New York. There Ramage was appointed a second lieutenant in the City Militia, was a freemason and a member of the New York Marine Society. On 29 January 1787, in the First and Second Presbyterian Church, New York, he married Catherine Collins; they were to have two sons and a daughter.

During his first ten years in New York, he lived in extremely affluent circumstances, and counted among his well known patrons Pintards, Gerrys, Ludlows, Van Rensselaers, Van Cortlands, McCombs, Rutgerses, and George Washington. Ramage's Washington portrait was commissioned by Martha Washington and is documented by George Washington's diary dated 3 October 1789, which mentions a sitting for Ramage. This particular painting shows Washington's head facing three-quarters left, with the order of the Cincinnati hanging from the left lapel of his coat. There are at least two other miniatures painted by Ramage of Washington: both depict him in full face, in uniform but without the order of the Cincinnati. The third portrait is in the Metropolitan Museum in New York, a bequest of the late Charles Mun. Ramage was a skilled goldsmith; the elegant cases he made for his miniatures complement the rich colours and delicacy of the portraits.

He left his family behind in 1794, when he fled to Montreal to avoid being imprisoned for debt; however, he was almost drowned en route, suffered from fever, and on arrival was thrown in jail by the British authorities as a suspected American sympathiser. He was imprisoned for a month, and on release attempted without much success to rebuild his career as a miniaturist. He died on 24 October 1802, and was buried in the Protestant cemetery in Montreal.

Elizabeth Frances Martin

SOURCES
Walter G. Strickland, *A dictionary of Irish artists* (2 vols, 1913; repr. 1969); Mantle Fielding, *Dictionary of American painters, sculptors and engravers* (1926), 293; George C. Groce and David H. Wallace, *New York Historical Society dictionary of arts in America 1564–1860* (1957), 522–3; *DCB*; Bernard Myers (ed.), *McGraw-Hill dictionary of art* (1969), 474; *ANB*; www.familysearch.org (accessed 2008)

Ross, Robert
1766–1814
Major-general

Robert Ross was born in Dublin, second son of Maj. David Ross of Rostrevor, Co. Down, a veteran of the Seven Years' War (1756–63), and his wife Elizabeth, daughter of Thomas Adderley of Innishannon, Co. Cork, and half-sister of James Caulfeild, 1st earl of Charlemont. Educated at home by a private tutor, Robert entered Trinity College Dublin in October 1784, graduating BA in spring 1789. In August 1789 he joined the army as an ensign in the 25th Foot and, transferring to the 7th Foot, was promoted to lieutenant in July 1791. In 1799, by then a major in the 20th Foot, he took part in the duke of York's expedition to Holland and was severely wounded in the action at Krabbendam (10 September 1799).

After service in Minorca he was promoted to lieutenant-colonel (January 1801) and served with the 20th Foot in the campaign in Egypt in 1801. Present at the storming of the French outpost at Ménou, he was given command of the 20th Foot in September 1803. In 1805 he served with Sir James Craig's expedition to Naples and Sicily, and played a prominent part in the battle of Maida, near the Straits of Messina. In July 1808 he took his regiment to Portugal and, serving under Sir John Moore, took part in the retreat to Corunna and the battle there (16 January 1809). In August 1809 he took part in the disastrous expedition to Walcheren, where his regiment suffered severe casualties from illness. After a period in Ireland, where the regiment was sent to recover, he returned to the Iberian peninsula at the end of 1812. He was given command of a brigade in the spring of 1813 and in June was promoted to major-general. Taking part in the battles of Pamplona and Nivelle (10 November 1813), he was severely wounded at the battle of Orthes (27 February 1814). Mentioned by the duke of Wellington in dispatches, he received the thanks of parliament for his services in the campaign.

In May 1814 he was given command of a brigade of infantry and sent to America as part of the expedition sent to stop the recent incursions by the American army into Canada during the War of 1812. Landing at Benedict on 19 August 1814, he led an expedition to the end of the Patuxent river, forcing Commodore Joshua Barney to destroy his flotilla of gunboats. Deciding to march on Washington itself, he engaged an American force of around 7,000 men at Bladensburg, the last defensible position on the road to the capital, on 24 August 1814. Commanding a force of just over 4,000 men, he attacked the strong American position; after three hours fighting, the Americans broke and fled. That same evening he led his troops into Washington and ordered that all buildings connected with government should be burned. That night the Capitol building, the White House, the treasury building, the war office, and the supreme court, along with other public buildings, were all burned. While the British government later maintained that this was in retaliation for American excesses in Canada, including the burning of York (Toronto) in 1813, the burning of Washington was condemned in the British press and by governments across Europe.

Deciding to march on Baltimore, Ross was leading his troops towards the outskirts of that city on 12 September 1814 when they were fired on by American sharpshooters. Ross was mortally wounded, a musket ball travelling through his right arm into his chest, and died two hours later. His remains were carried to Halifax, Nova Scotia, where he was buried, with full honours, on 29 September 1814.

He married (January 1803) Elizabeth Catherine Glassock (or Glasscock), who died in May 1845; they had several children, but only two sons and one daughter survived infancy. After his death, memorials were erected to him in Halifax, Nova Scotia, and in St Paul's cathedral, London. A royal warrant of 25 August 1815 allowed his wife and children to use the surname 'Ross of Bladensburg' in recognition of his services in the Peninsula and America. In 1826 the officers and men of his old regiment, the 20th Foot, placed a memorial in the church at Rostrevor, Co. Down, and also erected an obelisk on the outskirts of the town. There is a large collection of his letters in the Ross family papers in the Public Record of Nothern Ireland in Belfast. A fine oil portrait is in a private collection, while his sword and medals are in the Ulster Museum in Belfast.

David Murphy

SOURCES
Gentleman's Magazine, Oct. 1814, 401; B. Smyth, *History of the XX Regiment, 1688–1888* (1889); *DNB*; Sir [John] Bernard Burke, *Landed gentry of Ireland ...* (1912), 606; *Alumni Dublinensis* (1935); R. Horsman, *The War of 1812* (1969); W. A. Maguire, 'Major-general Ross and the burning of Washington', *Irish Sword*, xiv, no. 55 (winter 1980), 117–28; David Whitehead, 'David Ross of Bladensburg: a nineteenth century Ulsterman in the Mediterranean', *Hermathena*, clxiv (summer 1998), 89–99

Smith, James

c. 1713–1806

Lawyer, soldier in America, and signatory of the American Declaration of Independence

James Smith was born in the north of Ireland, second son of John Smith, a farmer with a large family. There are few details extant about his background or date of birth; he himself carefully concealed his true age. Around 1729 his father decided to emigrate with the family to America, where he joined his brothers in Pennsylvania. He settled in York County, and bought a large farm west of the Susquehanna river. Educated at Philadelphia, James studied under the Rev. Francis Alison before joining the law firm where his elder brother, George Smith, worked. He was called to the bar in 1745 and practised on the frontier in Cumberland County for five years before returning to York. His law firm was not a success, even though he had no competition, and in 1771 he engaged in an iron manufacturing speculation. It was not a success, and he bought himself out in 1778.

The impending conflict between Britain and the American colonies brought Smith to national prominence. In July 1774 he attended a provincial conference and read an 'Essay on the constitutional power of Great Britain over the colonies in America' that attracted much interest. In December he raised a volunteer company at York, and became its captain. When the company later grew to a battalion, Smith accepted the honorary title of colonel and was generally known as 'Colonel Smith', but never saw active service. Attending and speaking at provincial conventions and conferences during 1775–6, he made recommendations urging independence and drafted resolutions on this subject at the constitutional convention of 1776. In July 1776 he was elected to represent Pennsylvania in the first Continental Congress and became a signatory of the Declaration of Independence, although he had nothing to do with its writing. He was not selected for Congress the following year, but returned in 1778; he declined to sit thereafter.

Resuming his legal career as the War of Independence drew to a close, he served as a judge of the Pennsylvania high court of errors and appeals (1780–81), and as brigadier-general of militia in Pennsylvania (1782). In

1785 he was returned to Congress by the local assembly, but declined the honour because of his advanced age. Dedicating his final years to his legal career, he built up a large and successful practice. Smith was renowned not just for his impressive legal knowledge, but also for his wit and humour. He was an excellent anecdotalist; his awkward gestures and drawling mannerisms only added to the overall effect of his stories. He died on 11 July 1806 at his home at York. He married (1760) Eleanor Armor of Delaware; they had three sons and two daughters.

Patrick M. Geoghegan

SOURCES
Appletons; *DAB*; Mark Mayo Boatner (ed.), *Cassells' biographical dictionary of the American War of Independence, 1763–1783* (1966); Anthony A. Burdine, 'Colonel James Smith', *Irish Sword*, ix, no. 34 (1969), 47–9; *Who was who in the American revolution* (1993)

Sterling, James
1701–63
Writer and clergyman

James Sterling was the son of James Sterling, gentleman landowner, of Dowrass, King's County. He was taught by a Mr Lloyd in Dublin before entering Trinity College Dublin (1716), where he was awarded a scholarship (1718) and a BA (1720). His first play, 'The rival generals', was printed in Dublin and London in 1722 and performed at Smock Alley theatre, Dublin. The play, a tragedy set in the court of a Genoese doge, was not very original and was dramatically weak, but nevertheless it was one of the few plays penned by an Irish writer prior to 1740. In 1724 he contributed, along with Jonathan Swift and other Irish writers, to *Miscellaneous poems*, edited by his friend and fellow poet Matthew Concanen. During the 1720s Sterling and Concanen made a number of extended visits to London, where they hoped to establish themselves in literature. Sterling married (*c.* 1723) the actress Nancy Lyddal, who performed in Dublin and London, and in the late 1720s they lived in Darby Square, off Werburgh Street. Mrs Sterling was well known for her role as Polly Peachum in 'The beggar's opera' and gave a farewell performance in Dublin in 1732. Just after her death in that year, Sterling decided to take holy orders in the Anglican communion (he received his MA from Dublin University in 1733). He became chaplain to the Royal Regiment of Foot, but continued to pursue his literary interests. In 1734 he dedicated the *Poetical works of Rev. James Sterling* to the commanding officer of the regiment. Included in the volume is the play 'The loves of Hero and Leander', originally published in Dublin in 1728. Another play, *The parricide* (1736), was published separately in London. His poetical output, though mediocre, was very varied and ranged from a funeral poem on the death of William Conolly (1662–1729), speaker of the Irish House of Commons, to an 'epilogue spoken by Mrs Sterling on quitting the stage'.

In 1737 he received the royal bounty for going abroad as a Protestant missionary and arrived in America as a minister for All Hallows parish, Anne Arundel County, Maryland. He later became rector of St Anne's parish, Annapolis (1739), and finally rector of St Paul's parish, Kent County, Maryland (1740). In addition to his religious duties he also took an active interest in developing and protecting trade and industry in the colonies. He published *An epistle to the Hon. Arthur Dobbs* (1752), and in a sermon to the governor and assembly of Maryland (1755) he warned of the dangers of French encroachments on American soil. In 1751 he journeyed to England and tried unsuccessfully to obtain an exclusive grant for certain exports on the coast of Labrador. He was instead appointed by the crown to the position of collector for Chester and Patapsco, Kent County, Maryland (1752), despite opposition from both English and American trading interests. He held this position, which carried an annual salary of £80, until his death. Throughout his time in Maryland he contributed poems and articles to the *Maryland Gazette* and *American Magazine*.

Sterling did not make his mark in literary circles as he had initially hoped, but some of his surviving poems about the interaction between man and nature (e.g. whaling off Donegal and deforestation in the American wilderness) show that he could write strong descriptive passages. He was highly resourceful and managed to combine religious duties with more worldly activities such as the theatre and colonial trade, despite opposition from his more puritanical clerical colleagues in America. Natural business instincts and high-level contacts in England meant that he was able to gain preferment. While in America he witnessed first-hand the boom in the fur, whale, fish, and mast trade, and never let his clerical status prevent him from dabbling in commercial activities. He died in Kent County, Maryland, in November 1763. A long obituary appeared in the *Maryland Gazette*. He married secondly (1743) Rebecca, widow of the Rev. Arthur Holt, and had one daughter called Rebecca; he married thirdly (1749) Mary Smith.

Daniel Beaumont

SOURCES
'The dramatic writers of Ireland no. 1', *Dublin University Magazine*, xlv (1855), 46–7; *DNB*; Lawrence C. Worth, 'James Sterling, poet, priest and prophet of the empire', *Proceedings of the American Antiquarian Society*, xli (1931), 3–54; *Alumni*

Dublinensis (1935); La Tourette Stockwell, *Dublin theatre and theatre customs 1637–1820* (1938), 57–61; Peter Kavanagh, *The Irish theatre* (1946), 191, 266; J. A. Leo Lemay, *Men of letters in colonial Maryland* (1972); Patrick Fagan, *A Georgian celebration: Irish poets of the eighteenth century* (1989), 83–8; Edward C. Papenfuse et al. (ed.), *Archives of Maryland: historical list*, i (1990); Andrew Carpenter (ed.), *Verse in English from eighteenth-century Ireland* (1998), 253–9; *ANB*; Michael Glazier (ed.), *The encylopedia of the Irish in America* (1999), 880

Taylor, George
1716?–1781
Signatory of the American Declaration of Independence

George Taylor was born in Ireland, probably in the north of the country. His father may have been a clergyman or minister; the boy received a good education, but it is said that he was unhappy when apprenticed to a doctor. Apparently he ran away, penniless, and took passage to America as a redemptioner, arriving around 1736. His passage was paid by Samuel Savage, an ironfounder in Chester County, Pennsylvania, and the young man worked as a labourer at Savage's furnace for some time, until his employer realised that he could be useful as a clerk in the office. When Savage died in 1742, Taylor married the widow, Anne Taylor Savage, and ran the business until Savage's son died (1752), when changes were introduced by the remaining shareholders. Taylor moved with a partner to operate an important foundry at Durham, Bucks County, and then moved in 1763 to Easton, Northampton County.

He was successful in business, was elected a JP for the area, and in 1764 was elected to the provincial assembly, in which he served for five years. He was re-elected in 1775 and was a member of the committee of safety (1775–6), helping to draft instructions for delegates to Congress. Though not an extreme radical, he was in favour of throwing off British regal power, and he agreed to go as a replacement for one of the representatives of Pennsylvania in the Continental Congress of July 1776, who had opposed the Declaration of Independence. Taylor accordingly signed the declaration on 2 August 1776, or thereabouts, but seems to have resigned from Congress soon after he was involved in treaty discussions with Native Americans near his home in Easton (January 1777). In March 1777 he was elected to the Pennsylvania supreme executive council, his last public service. After six weeks, ill health caused him to resign, and he died on 23 February 1781 at Easton, and was buried in the Lutheran graveyard there. His house has been maintained as a museum.

Taylor and his wife (d. 1768) had a son and a daughter; the son had a family, but died before his father, and the daughter never married. With his housekeeper, Naomi Smith, Taylor had five illegitimate children. A likeness (which may, however, not be authentic) is in *Appletons*.

Linde Lunney

SOURCES

Appletons; *DAB*; *Who was who in America: historical volume 1607–1896* (1967); 'George Taylor 1716–1781' (www.colonialhall.com/taylor/taylor.php); 'Warwick furnace, Warwick, Chester County, Pennsylvania' (www.pa-roots.com/~chester/warwick_furnace.htm) (internet material downloaded Jan. 2005)

Tennent, Gilbert
1703–64
Presbyterian minister

Gilbert Tennent was born on 5 February 1703 in Vinecash, Co. Armagh, near Portadown, eldest son among four sons and a daughter of William Tennent (d. 1746), and his wife Catherine, daughter of Gilbert Kennedy. The younger sons included William Tennent (d. 1777). William Tennent senior was at the time of his son's birth a Presbyterian minister who was without a congregation. In 1718, along with relatives and other co-religionists in what is regarded as the first successful concerted migration from Ulster to North America, the Tennents travelled to Philadelphia, Pennsylvania. Gilbert was educated by his father in Ireland and America; a conversion experience in 1723 paved the way for his career in the ministry of the Presbyterian church, though he had originally planned to become a doctor. He was licensed by the Philadelphia presbytery in May 1725, in the same year that he received an MA from Yale college, granted despite the fact that he had not formally attended college lectures. He accepted a call to New Castle, Delaware, in December 1725, but was rebuked by synod when he left after only a few weeks. He assisted his father in his famous 'Log College' school at Neshaminy until he was ordained in New Brunswick congregation, New Jersey (1726).

His brother John Tennent (d. 1732), minister from 1730 of a congregation at Freehold, New Jersey, encouraged a revival of religious sentiment in his congregation, a revival that continued under William Tennent junior. Gilbert Tennent at first despaired of the state of grace in his own congregation, but with support from his father, brothers, and a Dutch pastor, Theodorus Frelinghuysen, he developed his ministry and preaching skills and began to see encouraging results among his hearers. The Tennents and the other graduates of the Log College increasingly came to believe that the religious life of individuals and of the community would only develop properly through personal conviction of sin, an awakening to God's grace, and a conversion experience validated by lasting and meaningful amelioration of behaviour and witness. Such was the level of personal involvement in the work known as 'the great awakening' that supporters of what came to be called the 'New Side' or 'New Light', often younger men, were happy to risk the censure of church authorities and the displeasure of colleagues by preaching unbidden in areas under the jurisdiction of ministers whom they regarded as less spiritually awakened. The revivalists were placed in a separate presbytery of New Brunswick in 1738, but this did not prevent them from sallying forth into other congregations and presbyteries if they felt it was requisite, even after an intrusions act was passed in 1739 in an effort to prevent unsanctioned incursions and divisive preaching and criticism. Tennent's fervour and eloquence were displayed to great effect when he joined the celebrated young English evangelist, George Whitefield, on a preaching tour in New England (1740). Tennent's joy in the work helped him forget his grief at the death of his first wife (name unknown) that same year; there were no children.

Tennent was pre-eminent among those involved in the revival in New Jersey and Pennsylvania; his appearance in the pulpit with unpowdered hair, and wearing generally a simple belted greatcoat, was particularly impressive. In March 1740 he made his most notorious attack on opponents whom he claimed had not experienced the work of the Holy Spirit, when he preached a sermon at Nottingham, Pennsylvania, on the 'Danger of an unconverted ministry'. His impassioned attack on 'Pharisee-teachers', and his declaration that hearers had the right to leave congregations they found unsatisfactory, did not endear him to ministers who were in sympathy with the 'Old Side'. The Tennents and their supporters were also strongly in favour of the kind of education provided in the colonies, in such establishments as the Log College, so long as the Holy Spirit could be seen to be involved, whereas opponents felt that only the long-established universities of the mother country, or Harvard and Yale in New England, could produce ministers of suitable academic standing. A split between New and Old Sides took place in 1741, when ejected 'New Side' ministers, following Tennent's lead, joined the New York synod. The schism lasted until 1758 and was the first serious division in the American Presbyterian church.

In 1743 Tennent accepted a call to a city congregation in Philadelphia, originally a non-denominational body founded because of Whitefield's preaching, which, after a split caused by the advent of the Moravian sect in the area, became the Second Presbyterian congregation. As a result of the split Tennent had to seek support from the wider community to finance the second church building. In this new setting he gradually adopted less controversial behaviour and began to find merit in the orthodoxies of his opponents. The onset of middle age may have diminished his radicalism, while he was increasingly concerned about the physical manifestations and other uncontrolled enthusiasm sometimes associated with revivalism and with Whitefield's preaching. After the Moravians, a sect noted for pietistic and emotional outpourings, arrived in America in 1741, he published a work criticising aspects of Moravian doctrine, especially their non-Calvinist promise of universal salvation. Ironically, he found the Moravians as disruptive in his own congregation as he and his supporters had been in former times in those of 'Old Side' opponents. Some former adherents accused him of back-sliding, but Tennent increasingly sought to find common ground with the 'Old Side', even with his most notable opponent, John Thomson (1690?–1753), also from the north of Ireland. In 1749, in his *Irenicum ecclesiasticum*, he praised Thomson's influential work, *The government of the church of Christ* ... (1741), and admitted that he now realised that early Christians had not dared to judge the state of grace of their fellow communicants. He also published sermons bearing the significant titles *The danger of spiritual pride* (1745) and *The necessity of studying to be quiet and doing our own business* (1744). Tennent so successfully exercised his leadership in the synod of New York that in 1758 it reunited with the synod of Philadelphia and he was elected the first moderator of the united synod.

'New Light' emphasis on the importance of local education for Presbyterian ministers led Gilbert Tennent to support the establishment of a state-supported College of New Jersey, which would be directed by Presbyterian ministers. In 1746 he was made a trustee, and from May 1753 to 1755 Tennent travelled in Great Britain with a colleague from Virginia, collecting several hundred pounds for the new college, later better known as Princeton University. His last few years in Philadelphia were made unhappy by the dissension in his congregation over whether he should retire in favour of an assistant, whose extemporaneous preaching made him more popular with the people; Tennent had begun to deliver sermons from notes when he moved to Philadelphia. He died on 23 July 1764; his death was announced two months later in his native Ulster, with the note that he had endured a 'tedious illness' (*Belfast News Letter*, 28 Sept. 1764).

Gilbert Tennent married secondly (9 February 1741), at Somerset, New Jersey, Cornelia Clarkson (née Bancker de Pyster), a widow with several children. She was of Dutch ancestry, ten years older than Tennent, and died in 1753. Before 1762 Tennent married another widow, Sarah Spofford, who had one daughter by her first husband, a Royal Navy captain. With Tennent, she had three children; one of the two daughters was given the name of Tennent's second wife, Cornelia.

Linde Lunney

SOURCES
Appletons; Ned Landsman, 'Revivalism and nativism in the middle colonies: the Great Awakening and the Scots community in east New Jersey', *American Quarterly*, xxxiv (1982), 149–64; Marilyn Westerkamp, *The triumph of the laity: Scots-Irish piety and the Great Awakening, 1625–1760* (1988); *Biographical dictionary of evangelicals* (2003); Family Search International Genealogical Index (www.familysearch.org); Marilyn Westerkamp, 'Division, dissension and compromise: the Presbyterian church during the Great Awakening', *Journal of Presbyterian History*, spring 2000; Tom Reid, 'Gilbert Tennent', online (www.evangelical-times.org/Articles/Feb03/feb03a03.htm); Peter J. Wallace, 'Old light on the New Side: John Thomson and Gilbert Tennent on the Great Awakening', (1995), online (www.nd.edu/~pwallace/thomson.txt); '*The Belfast News Letter* index 1737–1800' (http:///www.ucs.louisiana.edu/bnl/) (all internet material downloaded May 2006)

Tennent, William
1673–1746
Presbyterian minister

William Tennent was a son of John Tennent, a merchant in Edinburgh, and his wife Sarah Hume, and is believed to have been born in Mid Calder, West Lothian, Scotland, the family's ancestral home. Well educated, he graduated MA (1695) from the University of Edinburgh. Little is known of his early career; he seems to have been chaplain to the duchess of Hamilton, and may have gone to the north of Ireland in a similar capacity; the Hamiltons had huge estates and great influence there. He must have been ordained by a presbytery in Scotland, since in 1701 he was accepted as a minister by the general synod of the Presbyterian Church in Ireland; however, he was ordained in 1704 into the ministry of the Church of Ireland. Though he spent seventeen years in Ireland, he was apparently never beneficed; his children were baptised in several different locations in Ulster. James Logan, whose mother and Tennent's mother were related, advised him to emigrate to Pennsylvania, and the family travelled along with the first major exodus of Ulster people to New England in 1718. He applied to the Presbyterian synod of Philadelphia to be accepted by them as a minister. His petition very earnestly disavowed his anglican allegiance on theological grounds, but not surprisingly, synod took some time to be convinced of his sincerity. He was briefly a minister in New York, and then from 1726 in two congregations in Pennsylvania, one of which was at Neshaminy, twenty miles (32 km) north of Philadelphia, and in 1728 Logan gave him a land grant and £5 towards building a house.

Tennent continued the education of his own sons in Neshaminy and began to train others, following the pattern of similar establishments in

Ireland, where Dissenters, excluded from TCD, were often educated by Presbyterian ministers in country districts. A building to house the school was erected apparently in 1735; despite its modest size and construction (critics sneered at it as 'the Log College'), the foundation of Tennent's school has been described as 'the most important event in colonial Presbyterianism' (Trinterud, 63). It was important for several reasons: firstly, its very existence controverted the monopoly of Scottish universities and the handful of American institutions acceptable to the church authorities in training ministers; and secondly, Tennent's example was followed in various parts of the colonies by the men who had been his students. Presbyterian academies thus came to have a widespread, if not very long-lasting, educational dominance.

According to a monument erected on the site of the Log College, more than sixty schools and colleges, some subsequently very important, owe their origin, directly or indirectly, to Tennent's example. Samuel Blair (1712–51), his brother John Blair (1720–71) Samuel Finlay (1715–66), and Charles Beatty (1715–72) were four of the twenty or so graduates of the Log College, and Alexander Craighead (c. 1707–1766) may also have been there for a time. Thirdly, William Tennent in his Log College prepared the ground for the leadership of his four minister sons, Gilbert, William, John and Charles Tennent, in what became known as the 'Great Awakening', a revival of religious life and belief among colonial Protestants. The evangelical George Whitefield visited him, and compared his ministry in Neshaminy and the college to Goliath's sword. The 'New Side' held that the experience of a personal salvation was as essential for the ministry as for their hearers, and the Tennents, notable for their charismatic preaching and leadership, spread the message to their network of relatives and former fellow pupils. 'Old Side' opponents focused on the kind of education that the Tennents had experienced, and in the late 1730s controversy broke out about whether such men should be ordained if they had not had further training in the universities of Scotland.

This was one of the disagreements that caused the split in American Presbyterianism in 1741. By that time, Tennent had become infirm, and from 1742 no longer taught in his academy; it closed after Tennent's death on 6 May 1746. His marriage in 1702 to Catherine, daughter of Gilbert Kennedy, linked Tennent to several important dynasties of Presbyterian ministers and influential laymen in Ireland, and undoubtedly also in America. They had four sons and a daughter, all Irish-born.

Linde Lunney

SOURCES

Archibald Alexander, *The Log College: biographical sketches of William Tennent and his students together with an account of the revivals under their ministry* (1858, repr. 1968); J. G. Craighead, *Scotch and Irish seeds in American soil* (1878), 290–94; Guy Souilliard Klett, *Presbyterians in colonial Pennsylvania* (1937), *passim*; Leonard J. Trinterud, *The forming of an American tradition: a re-examination of colonial Presbyterianism* (1949), *passim*; *ADB*; John R. Muether, 'The story of Old Side Presbyterianism', *Ordained Servant*, v, no. 3 (July 1996); James H. Smylie, 'Neshaminy on our minds and hearts, 1726–2001', *Presbyterian Outlook*, n.d., online at www.pres-outlook.com/neshaminy.html (downloaded Nov. 2004); Tom Reid, 'Gilbert Tennent', *Evangelical Times*, Feb. 2003, information from Edmund Austin of Pennsylvania

Tennent, William
1705–77
Presbyterian minister

William Tennent was born on either 3 January or 3 June 1705 in Ireland, possibly in Co. Armagh, but more likely in Co. Antrim, second son among four sons and a daughter of William Tennent (1673–1746), a Presbyterian minister, and his wife Catherine, daughter of Gilbert Kennedy (1678–1745), also a Presbyterian minister. All four sons – of whom Gilbert Tennent (1703–64) was the eldest – became ministers. The family emigrated to America, possibly in 1716 but more likely in 1718, along with the first important emigration from Co. Londonderry to New England. William was educated by his father in what became known as the 'Log College' at Neshaminy, Pennsylvania, a first attempt to provide in America the kind of education required for ministry in the church. Overwork and religious fears broke his health, and in a state of emaciation and fever, while conversing in Latin with his brother about his soul, he fell down as if dead, and could not be revived by any means. The funeral was arranged, and only the importunities of his close friend, a doctor, saved him on two successive days from being buried. The assembled mourners were startled by a groan from the apparently lifeless body, and he eventually recovered, though he suffered long-lasting effects from the cataleptic trance, and had to relearn everything that he had once known. Years later, he was unable to describe accurately his near-death experiences, but the events were widely reported at the time, and an account by the celebrated Elias Boudinot (published in 1806 and several times reprinted) became very famous. Tennent stated that he had been in the presence of God; the groan which marked his return to life had arisen from his heartbreak at being told by a 'superior being' that he had to leave the ineffably beautiful scenes of praise and joy.

John Tennent (1707–32), a younger brother of William, had been since 1730 minister of a congregation in Freehold, New Jersey, where his piety and preaching had brought about what is regarded as the first instance in the mid-Atlantic region of the revival of religion known as the 'Great Awakening'. The graduates of the Log College, especially Gilbert Tennent, along with the itinerant evangelist George Whitefield, were for many years after 1729 instrumental throughout the colonies in producing emotional conversions and in seeking to increase religious fervour by fostering lay spirituality. After John Tennent's death from tuberculosis (23 April 1732), his bereft congregation chose William Tennent as their minister, and he was ordained in Freehold on 25 October 1733.

Earthly concerns held little interest for William after his life-changing trance; he neglected the congregational farm, and got into debt. When a friend suggested he marry a rich widow, Catherine Noble (née Van Brugh), he went to New York to examine her suitability, and in the first few minutes of their first meeting told her that since neither his time nor his inclination would allow him to use much ceremony, he would return on the following Monday to marry her and take her back to New Jersey. After some understandable hesitation on her part, they were married on 23 August 1738. Around the same time, he was accused by opponents of perjury when his testimony resulted in the acquittal of a fellow minister accused of theft. Tennent could produce no witnesses to clear his name, and conviction appeared inescapable till he was accosted on his way to court by two people from Maryland, who had been either hosts or servants in a house where the ministers had stayed. A dream three times repeated, which they had both had, warned them to travel to Trenton, New Jersey, where they were needed to help the Rev. Tennent; the alibi they provided ensured that the sermon Tennent had prepared to deliver while standing in the stocks was not required. Another well-authenticated story about Tennent records his waking with excruciating pain in one foot to discover that several toes were missing, having been cut off. At the time it was regarded as a supernatural occurrence, perhaps an attack by the devil.

Tennent strongly supported the 'New Side' in religion, preaching the need for revived religious life, and is credited with strong support for America's political liberties and said to have been influential in encouraging revolutionary ideas. He died in Freehold, on 8 March 1777.

The meeting-house that was built in William Tennent's time is an important historical site in New Jersey, and the congregation in 1920 adopted the name Old Tennent church. William Tennent and his wife (who lived till 1786) had three daughters who died as children, and three sons who died as young men. The eldest, John Van Brugh Tennent (1739–70), was a pioneer of obstetrics in America, and first professor of midwifery at King's College, New York, later Columbia University; he died of yellow fever in the West Indies. The middle son, William Tennent (1740–77), was an influential congregationalist minister in South Carolina, and a prominent politician in the state. He is credited with bringing about the disestablishment of the colonial Anglican church in South Carolina in 1777, and with preparing his hearers for some of the radical political developments of the revolution. He died of 'slow fever', which may have been typhoid. The third son, Gilbert Tennent (1742–70), also a doctor, was infected while inoculating patients against smallpox, but experienced a notable deathbed conversion.

Linde Lunney

SOURCES

W. Allen, *American biographical and historical dictionary* (1832, repr. in *British Biographical Archive (BBA)*); Archibald Alexander, *The Log College: biographical sketches of William Tennent and his students together with an account of the revivals under their ministry* (1851; repr. 1968); Allibone, repr. in *BBA*; *Appletons*; *ADB*; Marilyn Westerkamp, 'Division, dissension and compromise: the Presbyterian church during the Great Awakening', *Journal of Presbyterian History* (Spring 2000)

Thomson, Charles
1729–1824
Radical leader in pre-revolutionary Philadelphia and secretary of the Continental Congress

Charles Thomson was born on 29 November 1729 in the townland of Gorteade, in the parish of Maghera, Co. Londonderry, third child among five sons and a daughter of John Thomson, a Presbyterian linen bleacher, and Mary Thomson (née Houston?). In 1739 (after his wife died, possibly giving birth to Mary, who was the youngest child and only daughter) John Thomson emigrated to North America with Charles and three older sons: William, Alexander, and John. He became ill and died at sea. When the orphaned boys arrived at New Castle, Delaware, they were split up, and possibly were robbed or defrauded of whatever money they had with them. Some sources say that William Thomson (1727?–1796) a leader in the revolutionary war in South Carolina, was a relative, possibly an older brother. Charles lived for several years with a blacksmith's family; however, he ran away before arrangements were made for him to be apprenticed in the trade. It is said that a lady, impressed by his ability, helped him, and he made his way to New London in Chester County, Pennsylvania, to the home of schoolmaster Francis Alison, from Co. Donegal, a prominent Presbyterian minister and educator, who shared Thomson's Scots-Irish

Presbyterian background, and who can be regarded as a surrogate father for Thomson, the first of several who helped his career. Alison's school offered an excellent classical education and instilled in students an appreciation of the values associated with the Scottish Enlightenment; three other former pupils, contemporaries of Thomson's, were like him signatories of the Declaration of Independence.

In his last years at Alison's school Thomson assisted Alison by tutoring younger boys, before he set up his own school in Delaware. In 1750 he arrived in Philadelphia to take up an appointment as a classics master in the Academy of Philadelphia, starting on 7 January 1751. Francis Alison was rector of the Academy from 1752. In 1755 Thomson left the Academy for a teaching position at the Friends School in Philadelphia, where he spent five years. During Thomson's early years in Philadelphia, Benjamin Franklin became a close friend. Under Franklin's influence he joined other young Pennsylvanians, who discussed the ideas of the Enlightenment in a group called the Young Junto.

Franklin and Thomson shared a belief in the importance of practical knowledge; as Thomson wrote in his 'Plan of an American university': 'Learning should be connected with life and qualify its possessor for action.' Thomson combined his business and political activities with intellectual interests. He was the catalyst for the formation of the American Society for Promoting and Propagating Useful Knowledge. It was established in Philadelphia, with corresponding members in all of the colonies, and later merged with the American Philosophical Society in 1768, with Franklin as its absentee president. The society helped establish an independent American intellectual life in the colonies, and Thomson's varied scientific and scholarly interests are evident in its archives. The society also provided an opportunity for Thomson's rapprochement with Franklin, after their friendship had cooled over politics.

He spent two years (1757–8) working for Teedyuscung, leader of the Delaware nation of Native Americans, examining the history of that people's dealings with European settlers from William Penn's treaty with them in 1722. Thomson's anonymous *An enquiry into the causes of the alienation of the Delaware and Shawanese Indians from the British interest* (1759) concluded that later treaties, after Penn's time, had defrauded the Delaware Indians, and he criticised the policy of the current proprietors. Thomson worked on behalf of the Delaware people, acting as secretary in their dealings with officials, till the month-long meeting (October 1758) at Easton, Pennsylvania, to deal with the rival French and Indian claims over the frontier at Fort Duquesne (Pittsburgh). Thompson was adopted as a member of the Delaware nation during that month. Evaluating his work with the Delawares, Thomson's biographer Boyd Stanley Schlenther suggests that it was Franklin who convinced Thomson 'to change his views on Indian affairs to suit larger political goals' (p. 45). He gave up his work with the Delawares to open a dry goods shop near Franklin's home, at 324 Market Street, Philadelphia, but undoubtedly the experience with the Delawares influenced his thinking about resisting the power of a political authority. In later life Thomson expressed abhorrence of slavery.

It is not easy to trace Thomson's career from the late 1750s to the 1770s because he destroyed his correspondence and papers dating from that period, but it is known that the passing of the Stamp Act (May 1765) prompted him to make an early stand against taxation. It was not simply that the act imposed a tax on business transactions. Thomson's letter of 24 September 1765 to Franklin in London indicates that he felt that the Stamp Act was just the first shot fired in a wider attack on colonists' rights. Franklin, who had hitherto failed to appreciate the strength of North American reaction to the act, advised Thomson: '… let us make as good a night of it as we can. We can still light candles.' Thomson responded: 'The sun of liberty is indeed fast setting, if not down already, in the American colonies' (Franklin, xii, 207, 279, 178 n. 5). Parts of the exchange were made public when they were reprinted in the *London Chronicle*, 14–16 November 1765.

Thomson became a leading organiser of the Philadelphia protests against the Stamp Act. John Adams (1735–1826; second US president, 1797–1801) called Thomson 'the Sam Adams of Pennsylvania' (after Sam Adams (1722–1803), a radical Boston revolutionary). Thomson served as a delegate to the Stamp Act Congress that met in New York in the summer of 1765. The colonists' resistance and Franklin's advocacy of their views led to the repeal of the act in March 1766. Thomson's letter to Franklin (20 May 1766), thanking him for his work for repeal, assured Franklin that the colonists were still loyal subjects; however, as events unfolded, the repeal of the act was to lead to the first Continental Congress and the beginning of the united effort that would end with independence from Great Britain.

Thomson suffered financial reverses in the late 1760s. For a short time he owned a distillery business and managed an iron works outside Philadelphia, but continued to be a political agitator who urged colonists to buy only American products and boycott British goods. Keeping in close touch with the radicals in Boston, and heedless of personal safety, he began to urge that representatives of the colonies should gather in Philadelphia to discuss their grievances. The first Continental Congress opened on 18 July 1774. The conservative Pennsylvanian Joseph Galloway, who would become the civilian administrator for the British when they occupied Philadelphia, blocked Thomson's selection as a delegate from Pennsylvania to the Congress, but Thomson was elected its secretary. He was to serve the Congress for almost fifteen years till the federal government came to power in 1789. From the beginning, Thomson kept Franklin apprised of congressional deliberations, and sent to him a copy of their petition to George III with their list of grievances. In March 1775 he told Franklin that the colonies believed that their safety lay in their union. The following month the opening shots of the American revolution were fired in Lexington, Massachusetts (19 April 1775). The second Continental Congress opened in September, assumed charge of the military campaign, and drew up their manifesto, the Declaration of Independence. On 4 July 1776 Thomson and John Hancock, president of the Continental Congress, were the only two signatories of the original declaration; delegates signed a later copy, but Thomson's signature does not appear on that document.

Thomson continued to serve as secretary after the revolutionary war, while the Congress created a government that balanced the powers of states and a national government, first with the articles of confederation (1781), and later with the federal constitution, produced by the Philadelphia convention of 1787. His contribution in recording congressional debates and in influencing discussion and decision-making was unique in the early years of the republic. He drew no salary for the first year, but was awarded a large solid silver tea urn in recognition of his services. As well as his secretarial duties, Thomson was responsible for finalising the design of the great seal of the United States, adopted by the Continental Congress on 20 July 1782, and still in use. The motto of the new United States, 'E pluribus unum', expressed Thomson's belief in the importance of unity.

When George Washington's first government came into power in 1789, Thomson hoped to be elected senator from Pennsylvania, but he had made enemies, and was not elected to any office. He retired, somewhat resentfully, to the life of a gentleman farmer, on an estate belonging to his second wife, and corresponded with Thomas Jefferson about their shared scientific interests. He completed a history of the revolution, but – unfortunately for historians – decided against publication and destroyed his notes and manuscript. He finally returned to his early interests in the study of the classics and to his project of making the first American translation of the Old Testament from the Greek Septuagint text (1809). While the resulting translation impressed some scholars, his failure to provide a preface, as he had been advised to do, left readers without information about the original text and about his translation methods. The volume was not a financial success. A second translation project with a preface, *A synopsis of the four evangelists: or, A regular history of the conception, birth, doctrine, miracles, death, resurrection and ascension of Jesus Christ in the words of the evangelists* appeared in 1815. Eight years before his death, Thomson suffered the first of two strokes and spent the rest of his life in failing health and increasing senility. He died on 16 August 1824 at Harriton, Lower Merion township, Montgomery County, a few miles west of Philadelphia. He was buried first at Harriton, but his body was later removed to Laurel

Hill cemetery outside Philadelphia, where there is an impressive memorial.

Thomson married (1758) Ruth Mather. They had separated at some time before her death in 1770. It has been suggested that she suffered from depression after the deaths of their twin infant sons and may have taken her own life (Schlenther, 87). On 1 September 1774 he married Hannah, daughter of Richard Harrison and niece of the Quaker politician Isaac Norris. She was a woman of some means as well as spirit, who was 'read out' at her Quaker meeting for 'marrying out of meeting'. She died in 1807. Neither marriage produced surviving children, and property was left to nephews.

A drawing of Thomson in profile by Pierre Eugène du Simitière is in the collection of the Historical Society of Philadelphia. There are two portraits by Charles Wilson Peale: one painted when Thomson was about 50 (*c.* 1781) and one painted near the end of Thomson's life in 1819. Both are in the Independence National Historical Park Collection. A painting by Matthew Pratt (1794), which looks rather as if the artist painted Thomson's head above some other man's body, is in the Frick Art Reference Library. Thomson's papers are in the Library of Congress, in the Historical Societies of New York and of Pennsylvania, in the Sparks Manuscript Collection in the Houghton Library at Harvard University, and in the Princeton University Library. The papers of the Continental Congress, with Thomson's manuscript records, are in the National Archives, Washington DC.

Maureen Murphy

SOURCES
Appletons; Lewis R. Harley, *The life of Charles Thomson* (1900); George Corner (ed.), *Autobiography of Benjamin Rush* (1948), 289, 294; John J. Zimmerman, 'Charles Thomson, "the Sam Adams of Philadelphia"', *Mississippi Valley Historical Review*, xlv (Dec. 1958), 464–880; Benjamin Franklin, *The papers of Benjamin Franklin*, vii, xiii (1963, 1969), ed. Leonard W. Labaree; xxi (1978), ed. William Willcox; Cyril M. White, 'Charles Thomson: the Irish-born secretary of the Continental Congress, 1774–1789', *Studies*, lxviii (1979), 33–45; James E. Hendricks, *Charles Thomson and the making of a new nation 1729–1824* (1979); David N. Doyle, *Ireland, Irishmen and revolutionary America, 1760–1820* (1981); Boyd Stanley Schlenther, *Charles Thomson. A patriot's pursuit* (1990); *ANB*

Thornton, Matthew
1714–1803
Doctor and politician

Matthew Thornton was born on 3 March 1714 in the north of Ireland, probably close to Derry city. Details of his origins are somewhat vague: he may have been the third among five sons, and perhaps also had three sisters.

His father, James Thornton, said to have been married to Elizabeth Jenkins, emigrated with his young family, and possibly with his own parents, in 1717, or perhaps as part of the well-known organised emigration of 1718 from Ulster to the northern New England area. They settled first in Wiscasset, Maine, but soon moved to Worcester, Massachusetts, where Matthew was educated at Worcester Academy. After studying medicine at Leicester, Massachusetts, he successfully practised from 1740 in Londonderry, New Hampshire, in an area settled originally by Ulster Scots from Co. Londonderry and Co. Donegal. In 1745 he served as surgeon to the New Hampshire regiment during an expedition to capture Louisburg on Cape Breton Island from the French. He became a colonel in the New Hampshire militia, and as a prominent man in the community was made a JP and later chief justice of the court of common pleas in his county. He and other family members owned the land on which the township of Thornton, New Hampshire, was created in 1768.

Thornton's prominence locally and in the agitation against British rule led to his being selected as Londonderry's representative to the second Provincial Congress in January 1775; he was president of the fourth Congress in May 1775. He held at the same time the important post of chairman of the committee of safety, and was also chairman of the small committee that drafted a constitution for the province of New Hampshire. In January 1776 he was elected speaker of the fifth Congress, which adopted the constitution. New Hampshire was the first colony to adopt a constitution, and thus Thornton, along with his state, was in the vanguard of revolutionary thinking and political developments as the colonies moved rapidly towards breaking the link with Great Britain. He was sent as a delegate to the Continental Congress in September 1776, and although not present for the vote on the Declaration of Independence, was permitted to add his signature in November 1776 to the engrossed document which others had signed in July of that year. (There was though no room for his name alongside the other New Hampshire delegates).

He continued to be prominent in state affairs, and was until 1782 a justice of the state supreme court; from 1783 he sat in the state legislature. In 1786 he was a state senator, and retained that position until 1788, when he retired as a gentleman farmer to Thornton's Ferry on the Merrimack river in New Hampshire. From there he continued to send political essays to the newspapers; he died in Newburyport, Massachusetts, on 24 June 1803, while visiting his daughter, but was buried in Thornton's Ferry. His gravestone originally bore the simple epitaph 'An honest man', but was later made more elaborate. He is said to have enjoyed the confidence of George Washington, and to have been a tall, dignified and impressive man, whose unpublished manuscripts included a lengthy treatise on the origin of evil.

He married (1760) Hannah Jack or Jackson (d. 1786). They had three sons and two daughters; one of the sons died in 1787. A grandson, James Shepard Thornton, born 1826 in Merrimack, New Hampshire, was a prominent naval officer during the Civil War.

Linde Lunney

SOURCES
S. F. French, *Biographia Americana* (1825), repr. in *BBA*; W. Allen, *An American biographical and historical dictionary* (1832), repr. in *BBA*; *Appletons*; Charles Thornton Adams, 'The family of James Thornton father of Hon. Matthew Thornton' (1905), xerox copy provided by Jeffrey W. Card; Mark M. Boatner, *Cassell's biographical dictionary of the American war of independence* (1973); Della Gray Barthelmas, *The signers of the declaration of independence: a biographical and genealogical reference* (1997), 268–9; Peter E. Randall, 'Matthew Thornton', *New Hampshire: years of revolution* (1976); information from Jeffrey W. Card, family historian, posted on Thornton family forum at www.genforum/genealogy.com, message no. 1246 (internet material downloaded 24 Jan. 2001).

Waddell, Hugh
1734–73
Colonial general

Hugh Waddell was born in Lisburn, Co. Antrim, son of Hugh Waddell, a prosperous farmer, and Isabella Waddell (née Brown). His father killed a man in a duel and was forced to flee the country. Emigrating to America, Hugh was educated in Boston, Massachusetts, where he spent his early life. Returning to Ireland *c.* 1752, Hugh Waddell senior discovered that his estate had been seized, and realised he was penniless; his health gave way and he died soon after. Faced with few opportunities in Ireland, Hugh decided to go back to the colonies and settled in North Carolina, where his friend Arthur Dobbs had just been appointed as royal governor. Arriving in 1754 he was immediately embroiled in the impending conflict between the Virginians and the French, and enlisted in a North Carolina regiment being raised to assist its neighbouring colony. Commissioned a lieutenant, he soon proved himself an able and energetic soldier and was promoted to captain. In winter 1755, when he returned from active duty in Virginia, he was appointed clerk of the provisional council in North Carolina.

Given command of the colony's Ranger companies, Waddell was responsible for constructing forts at key strategic points between the Yadkin and Catawba rivers. One of the most impressive of these was named Fort Dobbs; another, Fort Waddell. Anxious to improve his soldiers' efficiency, he studied and adapted the fighting methods of the Native American peoples that he encountered. He also helped negotiate a provincial treaty with the Catawbas and the Cherokees in 1756; as a result he secured the use of Indian scouts who proved invaluable for reconnaissance in subsequent conflicts. As his reputation continued to grow, he was elected for four consecutive terms in the North Carolina general assembly (1757–60). Now a major in the army, he was given command of three companies of soldiers and played a critical role in the capture of Fort Duquesne (1758), removing French influence from the region. Tensions with the Cherokees soon erupted and he led a successful series of raids on them in South Carolina the following year; he also helped defend Fort Dobbs from assault in 1760. Purchasing much land in the area, and benefiting from the patronage of Governor Dobbs, Waddell established himself as one of the leading political and military figures in North Carolina. He served a further four terms in the general assembly (1762, 1766, 1767, 1771). In 1762 he married Mary Haynes, with whom he had three sons.

The death of Dobbs in 1765 did not prove a setback to Waddell's career. Waddell soon developed a close relationship with Dobbs's successor, William Tryon, but defied him to oppose the controversial British Stamp Act in February 1766, which he viewed as unconstitutional. After visiting Ireland in 1768, he returned to America to become general of the provisional militia. In 1771 he was involved in the war of regulations against frontier settlers who were campaigning against various injustices, but had his supply train captured in a skirmish.

Towards the end of 1772 his health failed and he died on 9 April 1773 at the Castle Haynes plantation, North Carolina. He was regarded as the leading soldier in the colony before the American revolution, and his death was a major loss for the colonial cause in its struggle for rights and, eventually, independence.

Patrick M. Geoghegan

SOURCES
Alfred Moore Waddell, *A colonial officer and his times, 1754–73: a biographical sketch of Gen. Hugh Waddell* (1885); *Appletons*; *DAB*; *ANB*; Michael Glazier (ed.), *The encylopedia of the Irish in America* (1999)

Warren, Sir Peter
1703–52
Admiral in the Royal Navy

Sir Peter Warren was born on 10 March 1703 at Warrenstown, Co. Meath, third son among three sons and two daughters of Michael Warren, a Catholic landowner, and Catherine Warren (née Aylmer). Educated locally, he entered the Royal Navy in 1716, under the supervision of his uncle Admiral Matthew Aylmer, and soon converted to Protestantism. Rising rapidly, thanks to his ability as well as to the patronage of his relative, he became a midshipman in 1719 and a lieutenant in 1723. Given command of the *Grafton*, he was made a captain in 1727, and stationed in the Baltic. In 1730 he was sent to America as captain of the *Solebay* and spent much of the next seventeen years based at New York. In 1731 he married Susanna de Lancey; they had one son and four daughters. His nephew was William Johnson (1715–74), whom he brought to America in 1738, and appointed as manager of Warren's extensive land holdings. Warren's home was at Greenwich House, on the Hudson river, and he owned 300 acres of what is now Greenwich Village.

Warren quickly amassed a large fortune, thanks in large part to the prize money he won in various naval encounters. With the outbreak of war with Spain, he commanded a squadron in Jamaica (1744), and the following year won many battles against the French. He commanded the British fleet at the siege of Louisbourg, Cape Breton Island (1745), and captured prizes that were estimated to total £1 million; Warren's share was the 'admiral's eighth'. Refused a baronetcy because he had no heir at that time, he was instead made rear-admiral and appointed governor of Cape Breton. Returning to England (December 1746), he was immediately dispatched to fight the French fleet at Cape Finisterre. He won a brilliant victory (3 May 1747) and became a hero in England; he was knighted and given command of the western squadron. Cashing in on his popularity, he ran for parliament and was elected for Westminster in 1747; his expenses, however, came to £7,000. On 12 May 1748 he was promoted to vice-admiral but ill-health prevented him from returning to active service. Believed by contemporaries to be the richest commoner in Britain, he invested his money carefully, engaged in various philanthropic ventures, and purchased a large estate, Westbury, in Hampshire. In parliament he unwisely attached his fortunes to the Prince of Wales, and when the prince died (1751) Warren was left without a patron.

Warren died on 29 July 1752 in Dublin of a violent fever, while on a visit to purchase some estates in Ireland. He was buried near his birthplace at Warrenstown, and a large monument was erected in his honour at Westminster Abbey.

Patrick M. Geoghegan

SOURCES
DNB; *DAB*; R. Sedgwick, *The history of parliament: the house of commons, 1715–54* (1970); *DCB*; Julian Gwyn, *The enterprising admiral: the personal fortune of Admiral Sir Peter Warren* (1974); *North Munster Antiquarian Journal*, xvii (1975), 60; *ANB*.

Personal name index

This index includes the names of women mentioned in the articles; the married surname is used as the headword form, with links from birth surnames and the names of re-married widows also included. This will add to the interest of the index for family historians, and is moreover an attempt to represent the contribution of women to Irish and American colonial history.

Place-name index

Image credits

Library of Congress (John Barry); National Gallery of Art (Guy Johnson); National Portrait Gallery (George Berkeley); New York Public Library (engraving by John James Barralet, Anne Bonney, Sir Guy Carleton, Arthur Dobbs, John Dunlap, engraving of Philip Embury's church, Samuel Finley, Hugh Gaine, Barbara Heck, Charles Inglis, William Irvine, drawing of Fort Johnson, Sir William Johnson, James Logan, James MacSparran, Richard Montgomery, William Paterson, William Penn, James Smith, George Taylor, Matthew Thornton, Hugh Waddell, Sir Peter Warren); New-York Historical Society (Thomas Dongan); Presbyterian Historical Society, Philadelphia (Francis Alison, Ogden painting of Francis Makemie before Lord Cornbury); William Roulston (photographs of headstone of James McGregor, General Robert Ross monument, William Martin memorial, gravestone of William Boyd); Wikipedia Creative Commons (Thomas Fitzsimons).